The Art of Po

Poems Past & Pi
Relationships

Published by Peripeteia Press Ltd.

First published February 2017

ISBN: 978-0-9954671-3-2

Peripeteia.webs.com

Contents

General Introduction to the The Art of Poetry series

The philosopher Nietzsche described his work as 'the greatest gift that [mankind] has ever been given'. The Elizabethan poet Edmund Spenser hoped his book *The Faerie Queene* would magically transform its readers into noblemen. In comparison, our aims for *The Art of Poetry* series of books are a little more modest. Fundamentally we aim to provide books that will be of maximum use to English students and their teachers. In our experience, few students read essays on poems, yet, whatever specification they are studying, they have to write analytical essays on poetry. So, we've offering some models, written in a lively and accessible style. We believe too that the essay as a form in itself needs championing, especially when so many revision books for students present information in broken down note form.

For Volume 1 we chose canonical poems for several reasons: Firstly, they are simply great poems, well worth reading and studying; secondly, we chose poems from across time so that they sketch in outline major developments in English poetry, from the Elizabethan period up until the present day, so that the volume works as an introduction to poetry and poetry criticism. And, being canonical poems, this selection often crops up on GCSE and A-level specifications, so our material will be useful critical accompaniment and revision material. Our popular volumes 2-5 focused on poems set at A-level by the Edexcel and AQA boards respectively. In this current volume and its partner, volume 7, we turn our focus back to GCSE, providing critical support for students reading AQA's poetry anthology, and, in particular, those aiming to reach the very highest grades.

1

Introduction to *Volume 7*: Love & Relationships

An adventure into what one apprehends

When writing about themes, students often simply state what they think the major theme of a poem to be. As AQA has kindly arranged these poems as a thematic cluster, writing something like 'this is a poem about love and relationships' doesn't get us very far. Sometimes readers also labour under a misconception about the nature of poetry, believing that poems have secret messages that poets annoyingly have hidden under deliberately obscure language. The task of the reader becomes to decode the obscure language and extract this buried message. Unsurprisingly, this misconception of poetry as a sort of fancy subcategory of fables makes readers wonder why poets went to all the irritating trouble of hiding their messages in the first place. If they had something to say, why didn't the poet just say it and save everyone a lot of unnecessary fuss and bother? Why couldn't Browning, for instance, have just said that rich, powerful men can be abusive monsters?

The Romantic poet, John Keats's comment about distrusting poetry that has a 'palpable design' on the reader has been much quoted. For Keats, and many poets, a 'palpable design' is an aspect of rhetoric and particularly of propaganda and a poem is not just a piece of propaganda for a poet's ideas. As the modern poet, George Szirtes puts it, poems are not 'rhymed advertisements for the already formed views of poets'. Here's George discussing the issue: 'A proper poem has to be a surprise: no surprise for the poet no surprise for the reader, said Robert Frost and I think that he and Keats were essentially right. A proper poem should arise out of a naked unguarded experience that elicits surprise in the imagination by extending the consciousness in some way. Poetry is not what one knows but an adventure into what one apprehends.'[1]

Most poems are not merely prettified presentations of a poet's preformed views about a particular theme or issue; they are more like thought experiments or journeys of exploration and discovery. In other words, poetry, like all art, is equipment for thinking and feeling. So, instead of writing that 'poem x is about love and relationships' try to think more carefully through what is interesting or unusual or surprising about the poem's exploration of these subjects. Sometimes the nature of the love or the central relationship will be obvious, as in poems exploring romantic love; at other times the type of love might be more unusual or crop up in an incongruous context. Approach a poem with questions in mind: What does the poem have to say about its theme? What angle does the poet take; is the poem celebratory, mournful, exploratory? To what extent does the poem take up arms and argue for something and have a 'palpable design'? Is their attitude to the subject consistent or does it change? To what extent is the poem philosophical or emotional? Do we learn something new, does it change how we think or feel? How might the poem have extended our thinking about its subject?

It would be trite to conclude that all these various poems are merely telling us that love is a wonderful thing and that good relationships are central to a fulfilling life. Love spurned, after all, can curdle into hate. Love for one person, nation or idea can lead to antipathy towards other people, nations or ideas. Are there any poems in AQA's anthology critiquing love? Are there any instances of destructive, jealous or unhealthy relationships in these

---

[1] http://georgeszirtes.blogspot.co.uk/

poems? Of course there are. Are there any unusual or counterintuitive manifestations of love and relationships? The madness of love? The selfishness or cruelty of love? Relationships as constraining and oppressive? Is the love between two lovers or does the poem depict platonic or familial love? Is the poem a meditation on the nature of love or a powerful expression of the experience of being in love? We're sure you get the idea. A key thing to remember is that 'love' is both a feeling and an idea. And ideas of love change over time and space. An adventure into what you apprehend is a great way to conceptualise a poem. And it's very productive too as a way to think about writing poetry criticism.

How to analyse a poem (seen or unseen)

A list of ingredients, not a recipe

Firstly, what not to do: sometimes pupils have been so programmed to spot poetic features such as alliteration that they start analysis of a poem with close reading of these micro aspects of technique. This is never a good idea. A far better strategy is to begin by trying to develop an overall understanding of what the poem is about. Once this has been established, you can then delve into the poem's interior, examining its inner workings through the frame of your hypothesis. And you should be flexible enough to adapt, refine or even reject this hypothesis in the light of your investigation. The essential thing is to make sure that whether you're discussing imagery or stanza form, sonic effects or syntax, enjambment or vocabulary, you always explore the significance of the feature in terms of meanings and effect.

Someone once compared texts to cakes. When you're presented with a cake the first thing you notice is what it looks like. Probably the next thing you'll do is taste it and find out if you like the flavour. This aesthetic experience will come first. Only later might you investigate the ingredients and how it was made. Adopting a uniform reading strategy is like a recipe; it sets out what you must, do step by step, in a predetermined order. This can be helpful, especially when you start reading and analysing poems. Hence in our first volume in *The Art of Poetry* series we explored each poem under the same subheadings of narrator, characters, imagery, patterns of sound, form & structure and contexts, and all our essays followed essentially the same direction. Of course, this is a reasonable strategy for reading poetry and will stand you in good stead. However, this present volume takes a different, more flexible approach, because this book is designed for students aiming for levels 7 to 9, or A to A* in old currency, and to reach the highest levels your work needs to be a bit more conceptual, critical and individual. AQA's assessment objectives for this paper, for instance, emphasise the need for 'critical' and 'exploratory' engagement with the poems. Top grade responses will also include 'fine-grained analysis of language, form and structure' informed by a 'conceptualised approach'.

Read our essays and you'll find that they all include the same principle ingredients – detailed, 'fine-grained' reading of crucial elements of poetry, imagery, form, rhyme and so forth - but each essay starts in a different way and each one has a slightly different focus or weight of attention on the various aspects that make up a poem. Once you have mastered the apprentice strategy of reading all poems in the same way, we recommend you put this generic essay recipe approach to one side and move on to a new way of reading, an approach that can change depending on the nature of the poem you're reading.

Follow your nose

Having established what you think a poem is about - its theme and what is interesting about the poet's treatment of the theme (the conceptual bit) - rather than then working through a pre-set agenda, decide what you honestly think are the most interesting aspects of the poem and start analysing these closely. This way your response will be original and you'll be writing about material you find most interesting. In other words, you're foregrounding yourself as an individual, critical reader. This most interesting aspect might be idea or technique based, or both.

Follow your own informed instincts, trust in your own critical intelligence as a reader. If you're writing about material that genuinely interests you, your writing is likely to be interesting for the examiner too.

Because of the focus on sonic effects and imagery other aspects of poems are often overlooked by students. It is a rare student, for instance, who notices how punctuation works in a poem and who can write about it convincingly. Few students write about the contribution of the unshowy function words, such as pronouns, prepositions or conjunctions, yet these words are crucial to any text. Of course, it would be a highly risky strategy to focus your whole essay on a seemingly innocuous and incidental detail of a poem. But noticing what others do not and coming at things from an unusual angle are as important to writing great essays as they are to the production of great poetry.

So, in summary when reading a poem have a check list in mind, but don't feel you must follow someone else's generic essay recipe. Don't feel that must always start with a consideration of imagery if the poem you're analysing has, for instance, an eye-catching form. Consider the significance of major features, such as imagery, sonic patterns and form. Try to write about these aspects in terms of their contribution to themes and effects. But also follow your nose, find your own direction, seek out aspects that genuinely engage you and write about these.

The essays in this volume provide examples and we hope they will encourage you to go your own way at least to some extent and to make discoveries for yourself. No single essay could possibly cover everything that could be said about any one of these poems; aiming to create comprehensive essays like this would be foolish. And we have not tried to do so. Nor are our essays meant to be models for exam essays – they're far too long for that. They do, however, illustrate the sort of conceptualised, critical and 'fine-grained' exploration demanded for top grades at GCSE and beyond. There's always more to be discovered, more to say, space in other words for you to develop some original reading of your own, space for you to write your own essay recipe.

Writing literature essays

The big picture and the small

An essay itself can be a form of art. And writing a great essay takes time, skill and practice. And also expert advice. Study the two figures in the picture carefully and describe what you can see. Channel your inner Sherlock Holmes to add any deductions you are able to form about the image. Before reading what we have to say, write your description out as a prose paragraph. Probably you'll have written something along the following lines:

First off, the overall impression: this picture is very blurry. Probably this indicates that either this is a very poor quality reproduction, or that it is a copy of a very small detail from a much bigger image that has been magnified several times. The image shows a stocky man and a medium-sized dog, both orientated towards something to their left, which suggests there is some point of interest in that direction. From the man's rustic dress (smock, breeches, clog-like boots) the picture is either an old one or a modern one depicting the past. The man appears to be carrying a stick and there's maybe a bag on his back. From all of these details we can probably deduce that he's a peasant, maybe a farmer or a shepherd.

Now do the same thing for picture two. We have even less detail here and again the picture's blurry. Particularly without the benefit of colour it's hard to determine what we're seeing other than a horizon and maybe the sky. We might just be able to make out that in the centre of the picture is the shape of the sun. From the reflection, we can deduce that the image is of the sun either setting or rising over water. If it is dawn this usually symbolises hope, birth and new beginnings; if the sun is setting it conventionally symbolises the opposite – the end of things, the coming of night/ darkness, death.

If you're a sophisticated reader, you might well start to think about links between the two images. Are they, perhaps, both details from the same single larger image, for instance.

Well, this image might be even harder to work out. Now we don't even have

 a whole figure, just a leg, maybe, sticking up in the air. Whatever is happening here, it looks painful and we can't even see the top half of the body. From the upside orientation, we might guess that the figure is or has fallen. If we put this image with the one above, we might think the figure has fallen into water as there are horizontal marks on the image that could be splashes. From the quality of

this image we can deduce that this is an even smaller detail blown-up.

You may be wondering by now why we've suddenly moved into rudimentary art appreciation. On the other hand, you may already have worked out the point of this exercise. Either way, bear with us, because this is the last picture for you to describe and analyse. So, what have we here?

Looks like another peasant, again from the past, perhaps medieval (?) from the smock-like dress, clog-like shoes and the britches. This character is also probably male and seems to be pushing some wooden apparatus from left to right. From the ridges at the bottom left of the image we can surmise that he's working the land, probably driving a plough. Noticeably the figure has his back to us; we see his turned away from us, suggesting his whole concentration is on the task at hand. In the background appear to be sheep, which would fit with our impression that this is an image of farming. It seems likely that this image and the first one come from the same painting. They have a similar style and subject and it is possible that these sheep belong to our first character. This image is far less blurry than the other one. Either it is a better-quality reproduction, or this is a larger, more significant detail extracted from the original source. If this is a significant detail it's interesting that we cannot see the character's face. From this we can deduce that he's not important in and of himself; rather he's a representative figure and the important thing is what he is and what he isn't looking at.

Okay, we hope we haven't stretched your patience too far. What's the point of all this? Well, let's imagine we prefixed the paragraphs above with an introduction, along the following lines: 'The painter makes this picture interesting and powerful by using several key techniques and details' and that we added a conclusion, along the lines of 'So now I have shown how the painter has made this picture interesting and powerful through the use of a number of key techniques and details'. Finally, substitute painter and picture for writer and text. If we put together our paragraphs into an essay what would be its strengths and weaknesses? What might be a better way of writing our essay?

Consider the strengths first off. The best bits of our essay, we humbly suggest, are the bits where we begin to explain what we are seeing, when we do the Holmes like deductive thinking. Another strength might be that we have started to make links between the various images, or parts of a larger image, to see how they work together to provide us more information. A corresponding weakness is that each of our paragraphs seems like a separate chunk of writing. The weaker parts of the paragraphs are where we simply describe what we can see. More importantly though, if we used our comments on image one as our first paragraph we seem to have started in a rather random way. Why should we have begun our essay with that image? What was the logic behind that? And most importantly of all, if this image is an analogue for a specific aspect of a text, such as a poem's imagery or a novel's dialogue we have dived straight into to analysing this technical aspect before we're established any overall sense of the painting/ text. And this is a very common fault with GCSE English Literature essays. As we've said before and will keep saying, pupils start writing detailed micro-analysis of a detail such as alliteration before they have established the big picture of what the text is about and what the answer to the question they've been set might be. Without this big picture it's very difficult to write about the significance of the micro details. And the major marks for English essays are reserved for explanations of the significance and effects generated by a writer's craft.

Now we'll try a different and much better approach. Let's start off with the big picture, the whole image. The painting on the next page is called *Landscape with the fall of Icarus*. It's usually attributed to the Renaissance artist, Pieter Breughel and was probably painted in the 1560s. Icarus is a character from Greek mythology. He was the son of the brilliant inventor, Daedalus. Trapped on Crete by the evil King Minos, Daedalus and Icarus managed to escape when the inventor created pairs of giant feathered wings. Before they took to sky Daedalus warned his son not to get too excited and fly too near the sun as the wings were held together by wax that might melt. Icarus didn't listen, however. The eventual result was that he plummeted back to earth, into the sea more precisely and was killed.

Applying this contextual knowledge to the painting we can see that the image is about how marginal Icarus' tragedy is in the big picture. Conventionally we'd expect any image depicting such a famous myth to make Icarus's fall the dramatic centre of attention. The main objects of this painting, however, are emphatically not the falling boy hitting the water. Instead our eye is drawn to the peasant in the centre of the painting, pushing his plough (even more so in colour as his shirt is the only red object in an otherwise greeny-yellow landscape) and the stately galleon sailing calmly past those protruding legs. Seeing the whole image, we can appreciate the significance of the shepherd and the ploughman looking up and down and to the left. The point being made is how they don't even notice the tragedy because they have work to do and need to get on with their lives. The animals too seem unconcerned. As W. H. Auden's puts it, in lines from *Musée des Beaux Arts*, 'everything turns away / Quite leisurely from the disaster'.

To sum up, when writing an essay on any literary text do not begin with close-up analysis of micro-details. Begin instead with establishing the whole picture: What the text is about, what key techniques the writer uses, when it was written, what sort of text it is, what effects it has on the reader. Then, when you zoom in to examine smaller details, such as imagery, individual words, metre or sonic techniques you can discuss these in relation to their significance in terms of this bigger picture.

What would our art appreciation essay look like now?

Paragraph #1: Introduction – myth of Icarus, date of painting, the way our eyes is drawn away from his tragic death to much more ordinary life going around him. Significance of this – even tragic suffering goes on around us without us even noticing, we're too busy getting on with our lives.

Paragraph #2: We could, of course, start with our first figure and follow the same order as we've presented the images here. But wouldn't it make more logical sense to discuss first the biggest, more prominent images in the painting first? So, our first paragraph is about the ploughman and his horse.

How his figure placed centrally and is bent downwards towards the ground and turned left away from us etc.

Paragraph #3: The next most prominent image is the ship. Also moving from right to left, as if the main point of interest in the painting is off in that direction. Here we could consider the other human agricultural figure, the shepherd and his dog and, of course, the equally oblivious sheep.

Paragraph #4: Having moved on to examining background details in the painting we could discuss the symbolism of the sun on the horizon. While this could be the sun rising, the context of the story suggests it is more likely to be setting. The pun of the sun/son going down makes sense.

Paragraph #5: Finally, we can turn our attention to the major historical and literary figure in this painting, Icarus and how he is presented. This is the key image in terms of understanding the painting's purpose and effect.

Paragraph #6: Conclusion. What is surprising about this picture. How do the choices the painter makes affect us as viewer/ reader? Does this painting make Icarus's story seem more pathetic, more tragic or something else?

Now, all you have to do is switch from a painting to a poem.

Big pictures, big cakes, recipes and lists of instructions; following your own nose and going your own way. Whatever metaphors we use, your task is to bring something personal and individual to your critical reading of poems and to your essay writing.

Writing comparative essays

The following is adapted from our discussion of this topic in *The Art of Writing English Literature Essays* A-level course companion, and is a briefer version, tailored to the GCSE exam task. Fundamentally comparative essays want you to display not only your ability to intelligently talk about literary texts, but also your ability to make meaningful connections between them. The first starting point is your topic. This must be broad enough to allow substantial thematic overlapping of the texts. However, too little overlap and it will be difficult to connect the texts; too much overlap and your discussion will be lopsided and one-dimensional. In the case of the GCSE exam, the broad topic will, of course, be love and relationships. The exam question will ask you to focus on the methods used by the poets to explore a specific theme. You will also be directed to write specifically on themes, language and imagery as well as other poetic techniques.

One poem from the anthology will be specified and printed on the paper. You will then have to choose a companion poem. Selecting the right poem for interesting comparison is obviously very important. Obviously, you should prepare for this task beforehand by pairing up the poems (a grid to aid this preparation can be found at the back of this book). To think about this task visually, you don't want Option A, below, [not enough overlap] or Option B [two much overlap]. You want Option C. This option allows substantial common links to be built between your chosen texts where discussion arises from both fundamental similarities AND differences.

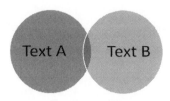

Option A: too many differences

Option B: too many similarities

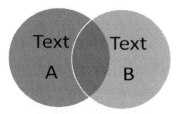

Option C: suitable number of similarities and differences

The final option will generate the most interesting discussion as it will allow substantial similarities to emerge as well as differences. <u>The best comparative essays actually find that what seemed like clear similarities become subtle differences and vice versa</u> while still managing to find rock solid similarities to build their foundations on.

Check the mark scheme for this question and you'll notice that to reach the top grade your comparison must be 'well-structured'. How should you structure a comparative essay? Consider the following alternatives. Which one is best and why?

Essay Structure #1

1. Introduction

2. Main body paragraph #1 - Text A

3. Main body paragraph #2 - Text A

4. Main body paragraph #3 - Text B

5. Main body paragraph #4 - Text B

6. Conclusion

Essay Structure #2

1. Introduction

2. Main body paragraph #1 - Text A

3. Main body paragraph #2 - Text A

4. Main body paragraph #3 - Text B

5. Main body paragraph #4 - Text B

6. Comparison of main body paragraphs #1 & #3 - Text A + B

7. Comparison of main body paragraphs #2 & #4 - Text A + B

8. Conclusion

Essay Structure #3

1. Introduction

2. Main body paragraph #1 - Text A + B

3. Main body paragraph #2 - Text A + B

4. Main body paragraph #3 - Text A + B

5. Main body paragraph #4 - Text A+ B

6. Conclusion

We hope you will agree that 3 is the optimum option. Option 1 is the dreaded 'here is everything I know about text A, followed by everything I know by Text B' approach where the examiner has to work out what the connections are between the texts. This will score the lowest marks. Option 2 is better: There is some attempt to compare the two texts. However, it is a very inefficient way of comparing the two texts. For comparative essay writing the most important thing is to discuss both texts together. This is the most effective and efficient way of achieving your overall aim. Option 3 does this by comparing and contrasting the two texts under common umbrella headings. This naturally encourages comparison. Using comparative discourse markers, such as 'similarly', 'in contrast to', 'conversely' 'likewise' and 'however' also facilitates effective comparison.

When writing about each poem, make sure you do not work chronologically through a poem, summarising the content of each stanza. Responses of this sort typically start with 'In the first stanza' and employ discourse markers of time rather than comparison, such as 'after', 'next', 'then' and so forth. Even if your reading is analytical rather than summative, your essay should not work through the poem from the opening to the ending. Instead, make sure you write about the ideas explored in both texts (themes), the feelings and effects generated and the techniques the poets utilise to achieve these.

Writing about language

Poems are paintings as well as windows; we look at them as well as through them. As you know, special attention should be paid to language in poetry because of all the literary art forms poetry, in particular, employs language in a precise, self-conscious and distinctive way. Ideally in poetry, every word should count. Analysis of language falls into distinct categories:

- By diction we mean the vocabulary used in a poem. A poem might be composed from the ordinary language of everyday speech or it might use elaborate, technical or elevated phrasing. Or both. At one time, some words and types of words were considered inappropriate for the rarefied field of poetry. The great Irish poet, W. B. Yeats never referred to modern technology in his poetry, there are no cars, or tractors or telephones, because he did not consider such things fitting for poetry. When much later, Philip Larkin used swear words in his otherwise well-mannered verse the effect was deeply shocking. Modern poets have pretty much dispensed with the idea of there being an elevated literary language appropriate for poetry. Hence in the AQA anthology you'll find all sorts of modern, everyday language, including some forthright swearing.

- Grammatically a poem may use complex or simple sentences [the key to which is the conjunctions]; it might employ a wash of adjectives and adverbs, or it may rely extensively on the bare force of nouns and verbs. Picking out and exploring words from specific grammatical classes has the merit of being both incisive and usually illuminating.

- Poets might mix together different types, conventions and registers of language, moving, for example, between formal and informal, spoken and written, modern and archaic, and so forth. Arranging the diction in the poem in terms of lexico-semantic fields, by register or by etymology, helps reveal underlying patterns of meaning.

- For almost all poems imagery is a crucial aspect of language. Broadly imagery is a synonym for description and can be broken down into two types, sensory and figurative. Sensory imagery means the words and phrases that appeal to our senses, to touch and taste, hearing, smell and sight. Sensory imagery is evocative; it helps to take us into the world of the poem to share the experience being described. Figurative imagery, in particular, is always significant. As we have mentioned, not all poems rely on metaphors and similes; these devices are only part of a poet's box of tricks, but figurative language is always important when it occurs because it compresses multiple meanings into itself. To use a technical term figurative images are polysemic - they contain many meanings. Try writing out the all the meanings contained in a metaphor in a more concise and economical way. Even simple, everyday metaphors compress meaning. If we want to say our teacher is fierce and powerful and that we fear his or her wrath, we can more concisely say our teacher is a dragon.

Writing about patterns of sound

Like painters, some poets have powerful visual imaginations, while other poets have stronger auditory imaginations are more like musicians. And some poems are like paintings, others are more like pieces of music.

Firstly, what not to do: Tempting as it may be to spot sonic features of a poem and list these, don't do this. Avoid something along the lines of 'The poet uses alliteration here and the rhyme scheme is ABABCDCDEFEFGG'. Sometimes, indeed, it may be tempting to set out the poem's whole rhyme scheme like this. Resist the temptation: This sort of identification of features is worth zero marks. Marks in exams are reserved for attempts to link techniques to meanings and to effects.

Probably many of us have been sitting in English lessons listening somewhat sceptically as our English teacher explains the surprisingly specific significance of a seemingly random piece of alliteration in a poem. Something along the lines 'The double d sounds here reinforce a sense of invincible strength' or 'the harsh repetition of the 't' sounds suggests anger'. Through all our minds at some point may have passed the idea that, in these instances, English teachers appear to be using some sort of Enigma-style secret symbolic decoding machine that reveals how particular patterns of sounds have such definite encoded meanings.

And this sort of thing is not all nonsense. Originally deriving from an oral tradition, poems are, of course, written for the ear as much as for the eye, to be heard as much as read. A poem is a soundscape as much as it is a set of meanings. Sounds are, however, difficult to tie to very definite meanings and effects. By way of example, the old BBC Radiophonic workshop, which produced ambient sounds for radio and television programmes, used the same sounds in different contexts, knowing that the audience would perceive them in the appropriate way because of that context. Hence the sound of bacon sizzling, of an audience clapping and of feet walking over gravel were actually recordings of an identical sound. Listeners heard them differently because of the context. So, we may, indeed, be able to spot the repeated 's' sounds in a  poem, but whether this creates a hissing sound, yes like a snake, or the susurration of the sea will depend on the context within the poem and the ears of the reader. Whether a sound is soft and soothing or harsh and grating is also open to interpretation.

The idea of connecting these sounds to meanings or significance is a productive one. And your analysis will be most convincing if you use several pieces of evidence together. In other words, rather than try to pick out individual examples of sonic effects we recommend you explore the weave or pattern of sounds, the effects these generate and their contribution to feelings and ideas. For example, this might mean examining how alliteration and assonance are used together to achieve a particular mimetic effect.

Writing about form & structure

As you know, there are no marks for simply identifying textual features. This holds true for language, sounds and also for form. Consider instead the relationship between a poem's form and its content, themes and effects. Form is not merely decorative or ornamental: A poem's meanings and effects are generated through the interplay of form and content. Broadly speaking the form can either work with or against a poem's content. Conventionally a sonnet, for instance, is about love, whereas a limerick is a comic form. A serious love poem in the form of a limerick would be unusual, as would a sonnet about an old man with a beard.

Sometimes poetic form can create an ironic backdrop to highlight an aspect of content. An example would be a formally elegant poem about something

monstrous. Browning's *Porphyria's Lover* springs to mind. The artist Grayson Perry uses form in this ironic way. Rather than depicting the sort of picturesque, idealised images we expect of ceramics, Perry's pots and urns depict modern life in bright, garish colours. The urn pictured, for instance, is entitled Modern Family and depicts two gay men with a boy who they have presumably adopted. A thrash metal concert inside a church, a philosophical essay via text message, a fine crystal goblet filled with cherryade would be further examples of ironic relationships between message and medium, content and context or form.

****

Reading form

Put a poem before your eyes. Start off taking a panoramic perspective: Think of the forest, not the trees. Perhaps mist over your eyes a bit. Don't even read the words, just look at the poem, like at a painting. Is the poem slight, thin, fat, long, short? What is the relation of whiteness to blackness? Why might the poet have chosen this shape? Does it look regular or irregular? A poem about a long winding river will probably look rather different from one about a small pebble, or should do. Unless form is being employed ironically. Now read the poem a couple of times. First time, fast as you can, second time more slowly and carefully. How does the visual layout of the poem relate to what it seems to be about? Does this form support, or create a tension against, the content? Is the form one you recognise, like a sonnet, or is it more open, more irregular like free verse? Usually the latter is obvious from the irregularity of the stanzas, line lengths and lack of metre or rhyme.

As Hurley and O'Neill explain in *Poetic Form: An Introduction*, like genre, form sets expectations: 'In choosing form, poets bring into play associations and expectations which they may then satisfy, modify or subvert'.[2] We've already suggested that if we see a poem is a sonnet or a limerick this recognition will set up expectations about the nature of the poem's content. The same thing works on a smaller level; once we have noticed that a poem's first stanza is a quatrain, we expect it to continue in this neat, orderly fashion. If the quatrain's rhyme scheme is xaxa, xbxb, in which only the second and fourth lines rhyme, we reasonably expect that the next stanza will be xcxc. So, if it isn't we need to consider why.

After taking in the big picture in terms of choice of form in relation to content

---

[2] Hurley & O'Neill, *Poetic Form, An Introduction*, p.3

zoom in: Explore the stanza form, lineation, punctuation, the use of enjambment and caesura. Single line stanzas draw attention to themselves. If they are end-stopped they can suggest isolation, separation. Couplets imply twoness. Stanzas of three lines are called tercets and feature in villanelles and terza rima. On the page, both these forms tend to look rather delicate, especially if separated from each other by the silence of white space. Often balanced through rhyme, quatrains look a bit more robust and sturdy. Cinquains are swollen quatrains in which the last line often seems to throw the stanza out of balance.

Focus in on specific examples and on points of transition. For instance, if a poem has four regular quatrains followed by a couplet, examine the effect of this change. If we've been ticking along nicely in iambic metre and suddenly trip on a trochee, examine why. Consider regularity. Closed forms of poems, such as sonnets, are highly regular with set rhyme schemes, metre and number of lines. The opposite form is called 'open', the most extreme version of which is free verse. In free verse poems, the poet dispenses with any set metre, rhyme scheme or recognisable traditional form. What stops this sort of poetry from being prose chopped up to look like verse? The care of the design on the page. Hence, we need to focus here on lineation. Enjambment runs over lines and makes connections; caesura pauses a line and separates words. Lots of enjambment generates a sense of the language running away from the speaker. Lots of caesuras generate a halting, hesitant, choppy movement to lines. Opposites, these devices work in tandem and where they fall is always significant in a good poem.

Remember poetic form is never merely decorative. And bear in mind too the fact that the most volatile materials require the strongest containers.

Nice to metre...

A brief guide to metre and rhythm in poetry

Why express yourself in poetry? Why read words dressed up and expressed as a poem? What can you get from poetry that you can't from prose? There are many compelling answers to these questions. Here, though, we're going to concentrate on one aspect of the unique appeal of poetry – the structure of sound in poetry. Whatever our stage of education, we are all already sophisticated at detecting and using structured sound. Try reading the  following sentences without any variation whatsoever in how each sound is emphasised, and they will quickly lose what essential human characteristics they have. The sentences will sound robotic. So, in a sense, we won't be teaching anything new here. It's just that in poetry the structure of sound is carefully unusually crafted and created. It becomes a key part of what a poem is.

We will introduce a few new key technical terms along the way, but the ideas are straightforward. Individual sounds [syllables] are either stressed [emphasised, sounding louder and longer] or unstressed. As well as clustering into words and sentences for meaning, these sounds [syllables] cluster into rhythmic groups or feet, producing the poem's metre, which is the characteristic way its rhythm works.

In some poems, the rhythm is very regular and may even have a name, such as iambic pentameter. At the other extreme a poem may have no discernible regularity at all. As we have said, this is called free verse. It is vital to remember that the sound in a good poem is structured so that it combines effectively with the meanings.

For example, take a look at these two lines from Marvell's *To his Coy Mistress*:

'But at my back I alwaies hear
Times winged Chariot hurrying near:'

Forgetting the rhythms for a moment, Marvell is basically saying at this point 'Life is short, Time flies, and it's after us'. Now concentrate on the rhythm of his words.

- In the first line every other syllable is stressed: 'at', 'back', 'al', 'hear'.
- Each syllable before these is unstressed 'But', 'my', 'I', 'aies'.
- This is a regular beat or rhythm which we could write
  ti TUM / ti TUM / ti TUM / ti TUM , with the / separating the feet. ['Feet' is the technical term for metrical units of sound]
- This type of two beat metrical pattern is called iambic, and because there are four feet in the line, it is tetrameter. So this line is in 'iambic tetrameter'. [Tetra is Greek for four]
- Notice that 'my' and 'I' being unstressed diminishes the speaker, and we are already prepared for what is at his 'back', what he can 'hear' to be bigger than him, since these sounds are stressed.

- On the next line, the iambic rhythm is immediately broken off, since the next line hits us with two consecutive stressed syllables straight off: 'Times' 'wing'. Because a pattern had been established, when it suddenly changes the reader feels it, the words feel crammed together more urgently, the beats of the rhythm are closer, some little parcels of time have gone missing.

A physical rhythmic sensation is created of time slipping away, running out. This subtle sensation is enhanced by the stress-unstress-unstress pattern of words that follow, 'chariot hurrying' [TUM-ti-ti, TUM-ti-ti]. So the hurrying sounds underscore the meaning of the words.

13 ways of looking at a poem

Though conceived as pre-reading exercises, most of these tasks work just as well for revision.

1. Mash them (1) – mix together lines from two or more poems. The students' task is to untangle the poems from each other.

2. Mash them (2) – the second time round make the task significantly harder. Rather than just mixing whole lines, mash the poems together more thoroughly, words, phrases, images and all, so that unmashing seems impossible. At first sight.

3. Dock the last stanza or few lines from a poem. The students should come up with their own endings for the poem. Compare with the poet's version. Or present the poem without its title. Can the students come up with a suitable one?

4. Break a poem into segments. Split the class into groups. Each group work in isolation on their segment and feedback on what they discover. Then their task is to fit the poem and their ideas about it together as a whole.

5. Give the class the first and last stanza of a poem. Their task is to provide the filling. They can choose to attempt the task at beginner level (in prose) or at world class level (in poetry).

6. Add superfluous words to a poem. Start off with obvious interventions, such as the interjection of blatantly alien, noticeable words. Try smuggling 'pineapple', 'bourbon' and 'haberdashers' into any of the poems and see if you can get it past the critical sensors.

7. Repeat the exercise – This time using much less extravagant words. Try to smuggle in a few intensifiers, such as 'really', 'very' and 'so'. Or extra adjectives.

8. Collapse the lineation in a poem and present it as continuous prose. The students' task is to put it back into verse. Discussing the various pros and cons or various possible arrangements – short lines, long lines, irregular lines - can be very productive. Pay particular attention to line breaks and the words that end them. After a whatever-time-you- deem-fit, give the class the pattern of the first stanza. They then have to decide how to arrange the next stanza. Drip feed the rest of the poem to them.

9. Find a way to present the shapes of each poem on the page without the words. The class should work through each poem, two minutes at a time, speculating on what the shape might tell us about the content of the poem. This exercise works especially well as a starter activity. We recommend you use two poems at a time, as the comparison helps students to recognise and appreciate different shapes.

10. Test the thesis that an astute reader can recognise poems by men from those written by women. Give the class one of the poems such as *Sonnet 29* without the name of the poet. Ask them to identify

whether the writer is male or female and to explain their reasons for identifying them as such.

11. Split the class into groups. Each group should focus their analysis on a different feature of the poem. Start with the less obvious aspects: Group 1 should concentrate on enjambment and caesuras; group 2 on punctuation; group 3 on the metre and rhythm; group 4 on function words – conjunctions, articles, prepositions. 2-5 mins. only. Then swap focus, four times. Share findings.

12. In *Observations on Poetry*, Robert Graves wrote that 'rhymes properly used are the good servants whose presence at the dinner-table gives the guests a sense of opulent security; never awkward or over-clever, they hand the dishes silently and professionally. You can trust them not to interrupt the conversation or allow their personal disagreements to come to the notice of the guests; but some of them are getting very old for their work'. Explore the poets' use of rhyme in the light of Graves' comment. Are the rhymes ostentatiously original or old hat? Do they stick out of the poem or are they neatly tucked in? Are they dutiful servants of meaning or noisy disrupters of the peace?

13. The Romantic poet, John Keats, claimed that 'we hate poetry that has a palpable design upon us – and if we do not agree seems to put its hand its breeches pock'. Apply his comment to this selection of poems. Do any seem to have a 'palpable design' on the reader? If so, how does the poem want us to respond?

'Poetry's a zoo in which you keep demons and angels.'
LES MURRAY

Lord Byron, *When We Two Parted*

A tryst

A cursory reading of Byron's *When We Two Parted* suggests a fairly typical, even clichéd, break-up poem, where the speaker reflects with sadness and laments a past relationship that failed to come to fruition. However, if we look at the poem more closely, we will see that the situation - and emotions expressed - are more complex and less clear than they initially appear.

The poem begins with the speaker recalling the ending of a relationship he was in years earlier. Despite the obvious significance of the memory, he seems to relate the incident with deliberate vagueness, and we are told very little about the lovers, who they are, where they are or why they are breaking up. The use of the pronoun 'we' implies there was something mutual about the separation and pain that was felt, with both lovers parting 'In silence and tears', as if something insurmountable and unspeakable had arisen to thwart their love.

In the second stanza we learn the break-up took place in the early part of the morning, which hints that they may have just spent the night together, and the 'chill' of the morning reflects the emotional coldness associated with the end of love, similar in effect to the 'winter day' of Hardy's *Neutral Tones*. Yet the semantic field of 'coldness' has already appeared earlier in poem, such as when the speaker recalls how 'Pale grew thy cheek and cold,/ Colder thy kiss'. This suggests an emotional coldness and detachment in the way the speaker's lover parted from him and there is more than a note of accusation and resentment to his words. The repetition of 'cold/Colder' accentuates the sense of hurt felt by the speaker, as does the alliteration of 'c' sounds in the words 'cheek', 'cold', 'colder' and 'Kiss', which creates a harsh sounding tone and almost a shivering or shuddering sensation.

As a whole the poem is written in *accentual verse*, a metre where every line of the poem has to contain a set number of syllables, in this poem two. Across the poem, the brevity of the two-stressed lines creates a terse and abrupt tone, as if we are listening to brief, loosely connected thoughts, which gives the poet the freedom to explore feelings in a more fluid and spontaneous way, also helping to create the poem's intimate and conversational feel. However, the line 'Pale grew thy cheek and cold' is one of only two lines in the poem where Byron breaks this pattern and includes three stressed syllables (pale, cheek and cold), the disruption in the poem's rhythm representing the break in the relationship as well as the speaker's sense of lingering on this detail and the subsequent loss of self-control. An acute sense of pain is also evident in the choice of 'sever' to describe the ending of the relationship, which connotes something like a limb being cut off suddenly and forcibly. The accusatory tone is also evident in the

description of the lovers as 'half broken hearted', the adjective 'half' indicating only one of them was really hurt by the separation, while the other was feigning or simply didn't care.

I hear thy name spoken

As the poem develops it gradually shifts from remembrance of the past to reflection in the present. This transition first occurs at the end of the first stanza where the enjambment of 'Truly *that* hour foretold/ Sorrow to *this*' [my emphasis], connects the past to the present by foreshadowing the renewed feelings of pain he is now experiencing about the relationship. Byron emphasises the importance of the link between past and present by making this the only other line in the poem that contains three stressed syllables. However, the shift from past to present is fully realized in the second stanza, where the memory of the early morning chill 'felt like the warning/ Of what I feel now.' Here we get the first full stop of the poem, marking a decisive change or break. Up until this point the poem has been following the rhyme scheme of a Shakespearian sonnet (*ababcdcdefef*). If the poem was a sonnet—a poetic form traditionally associated with love—we would now expect the poem to find fulfilment and conclusion with a final rhyming couplet (*gg*). Instead, the poem pushes on with its alternating pairs of rhymes, as if the rhymes, and by implication, the two lovers, are doomed to never find harmony or completeness with each other.

So what has happened in the present that has so forcefully shocked the speaker out of his peace and sent his thoughts cascading back into the memory of a break-up that happened years earlier? The answer lies at the end of the second stanza where the speaker reveals how 'I hear thy name spoken/ And share in its shame'. The sibilance of 's' and 'sh' sounds creates a whispering effect in the poem as if we are overhearing gossip about the speaker's ex-lover, indicating something secretive and illicit. A secretive atmosphere to the poem has already been established by the deliberate vagueness of the opening and the 'silence' in which the lovers departed from each other, but, at this point, a little background knowledge is helpful to shed light upon the poem. Around 1813, Byron conducted an affair with a married woman, Lady Frances Wedderburn Webster. The affair came to an end, possibly to avoid it being discovered, and both parties moved on with their lives. However, in 1816, it became public knowledge and a scandal that Lady Frances was having an affair with the Duke of Wellington. Byron, having overheard the rumours about his ex-lover, wrote this poem in response, although he dated it as having been written in 1808 to prevent people from working out who he was really writing about.

The harm done to the woman's reputation in the poem is acknowledged by the speaker who notes how now 'light is thy fame'. Lightness here suggests a lack of substance or weight, something that is now weak and no longer fixed in one place; the implication is that her indiscretions are known by everybody and her reputation is in tatters. The speaker 'shares in her shame' because he too conducted an affair with her and 'knew thee too well' in the Biblical sense of knowing/having a sexual relationship. His indiscretions with her though are unknown to others, who 'know not I knew thee'. However, the hearing of her name being gossiped about has a profound and painful effect on the speaker and her name is now 'A knell to mine ear;/ A shudder comes o'er me'. Byron uses the metaphor of a bell knelling, which normally indicated a death or

funeral, to emphasise either how the woman is dead to the speaker, their relationship has died, or that a part of the speaker has died. However it is intended, the pain and grief is acutely felt. The 'shudder' also seems to connect the present experience with the coldness of the woman and setting in the first two stanzas, reconnecting once again the past with the present. What seems to most grieve the speaker is that 'Thy vows are all broken'. Vows suggests wedding vows, but it would be rather hypocritical of the speaker to condemn the woman for breaking her wedding vows given that he also had an affair with her. What is more likely is that he is talking about the vows she made to him when they were together, perhaps promises of a future together or undying love. Now he hears of her affair with another man he feels betrayed.

By using the language of wedding vows to describe the relationship between them, the speaker reveals the depth of feelings and commitment he felt that they shared for each other in the past. But this present revelation about her now causes him to question and re-evaluate everything that passed between them when he asks 'Why wert thou so dear?' Is the rhetorical question meant cynically as an indication of disbelief he could ever have had feelings for her, or is it a genuine attempt to consider what was it about her that made her so special, which would imply he still has feelings for her even if he is not acknowledging them. What he does admit is that 'Long, long shall I rue thee/ Too deeply to tell'. 'Rue' means to feel extreme sadness but also to feel regret and it seems that he wishes he had never got involved with her. Or is it that he regrets still having feelings for her? The repetition of 'long', the series of present tense verbs ['rue', 'comes', 'grieve'], and the repetitive rhymes of 'me' and 'thee' also signal his failure to disentangle himself emotionally from his lover.

How should I greet thee?

While the first three stanzas focused on the past and then the present, the final stanza imagines a future where the speaker sees his ex-lover once again. What would he say to her? How would he act? The final stanza is a bitter one. It starts with the same plural pronoun 'we' that was used at the start of the poem to establish the couple's relationship with each other (albeit a relationship coming to an end), but the next line reverts to the singular pronoun in 'I grieve' to stress how it is only one of them that feels any pain about what happened. What grieves the speaker most is 'That thy heart could forget/ Thy spirit deceive'. The accusatory tone returns as the speaker remonstrates against how little he meant to the woman, how quickly and easily she forgot him and turned her affections towards someone else. The speaker asks the question 'How should I greet thee?' if he happened to ever see her again and answers with the terse reply 'With silence and tears'. While the image of tears suggests ongoing pain, the silence and refusal to speak with her indicates anger at how he has been treated by her. Like *Neutral Tones*, the poem forms a circular pattern, returning us to where we started, suggesting the speaker is trapped in his feelings of love, regret and self-pity. Like *Neutral Tones* the poem seems to suggest that when relationships end, we may well move on, but perhaps we never truly get over them.

When We Two Parted crunched:

PARTED – SILENCE – HALF – SEVER – PLAE – COLDER – FORETOLD – SORROW – MORNING – CHILL – WARNING – NOW – VOWS – LIGHT – I – SHAME – NAME – KNELL – WHY – THEY – TOO – RUE – DEEPLY – SECRET – GRIEVE – FORGET – DECIEVE – IF – LONG – HOW –TEARS

Percy Bysshe Shelley, *Love's Philosophy*

Simple truth

Love's Philosophy is one of the simpler poems in the Love and Relationships Anthology, but this does not make it a weaker poem; its power and beauty lies in its simplicity. The poem follows a long poetic tradition where a male speaker tries to persuade an unnamed woman to start a physical relationship with him. Andrew Marvel's *To His Coy Mistress* is probably the most famous example of this type of poem, a poem which also demonstrates how this tradition is much more about the poet showcasing their wit and linguistic inventiveness in following simple premises through to logical conclusions, rather than presenting a serious argument intended to successfully seduce a real-life woman. Some critics have read Shelley's poem almost as a dramatic monologue, where, as readers, we are meant to uncover clues in the text that reveal an obsessive and manipulative speaker who will not take no for an answer from his victimized object of desire. Such an approach is certainly justifiable if you choose to adopt it in the exam, but I prefer to see the poem more as Shelley's own contribution to a self-consciously playful tradition, where he offers a simple lyric poem that expresses the speaker's gentle longing for the woman with whom he is in love.

A philosophy is a theory - often presented as a logical argument - that is intended to reveal some truth about reality that might also act as a guiding principle for behaviour. The title, *Love's Philosophy*, suggests that the poem will reveal the truth about love; however, in personifying 'Love' as something that possesses its own philosophy, Shelley also elevates Love to a kind of divine power whose laws we should obey. The argument of the poem itself is a simple, if not fallacious, one: all things in nature mix and connect with something else beyond themselves, therefore the addressee of the poem should also unite with the speaker and start a relationship with him. Like many Romantic artists, Shelley believed that the natural world contained profound insights and truths about life and existence which people could learn from and use to transform and improve human relationships and society as a whole. It is not a surprise that the poem draws on so many images from nature to make its point. In the first stanza, 'Fountains', by which he means springs, 'mingle with the river',

while rivers flow into 'the ocean' and the 'winds' mix with each other. The analogies from nature continue in the second stanza where 'mountains kiss high heaven', 'waves clasp one another' and even flowers do not disdain each other. The speaker extends the natural imagery to the wider universe to universalize his argument: 'Sunlight clasps the earth' and 'moonbeams kiss the sea'. The whole universe seems to be urging the speaker and his beloved to be together. Or, perhaps, urging his beloved to accept the poet's physical affection.

What is most striking about the speaker's use of natural images is the way he personifies nature through his use of verbs to show interactions and interconnections which become increasingly physical and sensual as the poem develops; 'mingle', 'mix', 'meet', 'kiss' and 'clasp'. Everything within the universe is alive and acts with a single conscious purpose, to connect through love with something beyond itself, so who are we to deny this universal impulse? It is an argument strengthened with another interesting feature of the poem's language, the semantic field of religion in words such as 'heaven', 'divine' and 'spirit'. A famous atheist who, as a student, was thrown out of Oxford University for his unconventional beliefs, Shelley is sometimes criticized as being hypocritical and disingenuous here, using religious language as an easy way to strengthen his argument or worse still, to manipulate a woman who might possess religious beliefs that he does not share or accept. However, Shelley's atheism was not what we might think of as atheism today, i.e. the complete rejection of any supernatural governing power in the universe. While he rejected the Christian notion of a personal, omnipotent God who existed outside of the creation he made, like many other Romantics, Shelley expressed pantheistic ideas whereby God became an impersonal force that could be found within nature and which held the universe together. In *Hymn to Intellectual Beauty* Shelley referred to this force as the 'spirit of beauty' and in *Love's Philosophy*, love itself is the power which flows through all natural things and causes them to connect with each other. Again, the suggestion is that it would be foolish for the lady to resist the universal force that drives and unites the universe together, or as he puts it at the end of the first stanza, 'Nothing in this world is single;/ All things by a law divine/ In one spirit meet and mingle - / Why not I with thine?' The speaker thereby raises the relationship itself to a divine and sacred act.

Two into one

The poem's true genius and beauty however, lie in the way its structure and form intricately create the sense of interconnectedness expressed in its argument. To begin, the simple two stanza structure of eight lines each emphasises the poem's message that, throughout the universe, distinct pairs unite to create a unified whole.

The poem's *abab* rhyme scheme also suggests how pairs link to together to form a new unity. It is interesting however, how the first and third lines of each stanza ('river...for ever', 'heaven...forgiven') only form half-rhymes, as if to suggest the poem, and by implication the whole universe, will not be properly complete and unified until the lady agrees to a relationship with the speaker. Shelley also uses enjambment frequently in the poem to accentuate the force of love that drives all things in existence to mix and unite. We see this for example in the first two lines where 'The fountains mingle with the river/ And the rivers with the ocean' - the enjambment reproducing the sense of the one thing flowing inexorably into another.

Repetition is another technique the poet uses throughout the poem to accentuate his message that everything in nature unites and therefore so should the speaker with his beloved. Many words are repeated twice to emphasise pairings and interconnectedness, such as 'mingle', 'river', 'heaven', 'sweet', and 'clasp'. 'Kiss' is actually repeated three times as if to show this word is the most important for the speaker as this is the end point of all of his arguments; he may also want to suggests that kissing is not something that brings completion and therefore an ending, but something that continues indefinitely. Polysyndeton (the repetition of conjunctions in close succession) is a special type of repetition Shelley uses in this poem where he repeats 'And' at the start of lines. The effect is again to imply the relentless force of love that moves through the universe and urges all things to connect. Alliteration is also used to repeats pairs of sounds in the poem, such as 'meet and mingle' where the alliteration aurally creates the mingling that the meaning of the words points to. Other examples are 'high heaven', 'flower...forgiven' and 'work worth'. However, the sound effect most repeated in the poem is the sibilance of 's' sounds in words such as 'fountains', 'rivers', 'winds', 'sweet', 'single', 'spirit', 'sister', 'kiss', 'clasp' and many more. This creates an intricate web of interconnecting sounds that holds the poem together, just as love holds the universe together; it is almost if we listen closely enough, we can hear the whispering force of love as it moves across the poem and the universe, compelling all things to unite and join together.

The final structural technique to note in the poem is Shelley's use of punctuation. It is surely significant there is not a single full stop in the poem. Love is a relentless force that does not stop in its quest to connect and unite all things. Instead of full stops, Shelley uses semicolons to join and create a connection between sentences that would otherwise be separated. However, towards the end of each stanza he uses a dash to indicate a strong interruption to flow of the poem and its thoughts; in other words, something is going wrong at the end of each stanza. He emphasises this problem by ending each stanza with a question mark, which throws the poem's arguments over the female addressee and waits for a response. By ending each stanza with a question, Shelley introduces an element of disharmony into the poem, emphasised by the short final lines of five monosyllables in each stanza which disrupt the poem's rhythm and the stanzas' sense of completeness and unity. It is only when the beloved answers the speaker's questions in the affirmative and finally connects with him that the poem, and by extension the whole universe, will attain completion. As the speaker points out at the end of the poem with typical hyperbole, what is the beauty of the universe worth to me if I do not have you? It is an argument unlikely to succeed in the real word, but in the life and structures of the poem, ingenious and beautiful nonetheless.

Love's Philosophy crunched:

FOUNTAINS – OCEAN – MIX – SWEET – NOTHING – DIVINE – MINGLE – WHY – KISS – CLASP – FORGIVEN – DISDAINED – SUNLIGHT – MOONBEAMS – WORTH - NOT

NB

Shelley's poem might raise the question of what could prevent the woman from uniting with her impassioned potential lover. A little research of Shelley's life, and loves, will suggest a few possibilities. What difference, for instance, would it make if the addressee were already married? Or, indeed, the poet? How persuaded were you by Shelley's rhetoric? To what extent does he use 'love' when he really means 'lust'? Write a response from the beloved. Either write in letter form, or accept the more demanding challenge of writing back in verse. Alternatively, write a poem called *Hate's Philosophy* – 'All things by iron law infernal/ in contrary spirits separate and clash'...

Robert Browning, *Porphyria's Lover*

A taste for the macabre

The psychotic minds of villains and murderers have always exerted an extraordinary fascination on the public imagination. We might think, for instance, of the nightmarish world of Shakespeare's *Macbeth* or that embodiment of fiendish and malign cunning, Iago, from *Othello*. As in fiction so in real life: Interest in the Victorian murderer, Jack the Ripper, continues to burn strongly a hundred years and more recent example from fiction would be Hannibal Lecter from *The Silence of the Lambs*. The murder mystery story is a staple of mainstream television, sometimes in its lighter 'whodunit' guise, but, as in Nordic Noir, often also in darker, more psychological forms. Recently BBC's police drama *The Fall* courted controversy with its presentation of a handsome serial killer.

If we are tempted to stereotype Victorian culture as sexually repressed, morally earnest and sober mannered, we should bear in mind the popularity of sensation journalism, lurid 'Penny Dreadfuls' and Gothic fiction. Like us, it seems the Victorians had a taste for the macabre. Cheap novels and journalism are one thing; poetry, however, is another thing entirely. For Victorian readers, poetry would have been associated with high art, refined sensibilities and elevated subject matter. Browning pushes at the boundaries of good taste and decency by having a crazed killer inhabit this usually rarefied literary domain. And worse than that, the poet does not just present us with a portrait of a murderer, he leads us into the warped interiors of his mind. Positioned as witnesses to a murder, the murderer takes us into his confidence, almost as if we are his accomplices.

A mask of composure

Browning's poem begins conventionally enough, with a description of the setting to establish an overwrought mood and atmosphere. Using the literary technique of pathetic fallacy, the outer turbulence of the weather expresses the disturbed mind of the narrator. The world of nature depicted here is as in conflict; the animating force of the wind [commonly a symbol of the will] tears at the trees and 'vex[es]' the lake. 'Sullen' and spiteful, nature is animated and driven by violent, vengeful impulses. And yet, apparently, this makes the narrator want to weep; he listens to the turmoil 'with heart fit to break'. What he craves is an end to all this conflict, he craves peace, tranquillity, stillness. In his own, warped logic this character is going to bring peace to the world. And not only to the world. Though we might guess the peace he really seeks is escape from the confines of own violent emotions, in addition to symbolising his mind, later we come to realise that this opening description projects onto the landscape the narrator's perception of Porphyria as a conflicted person. Hence, in his terms, her murder is an act of pity, bringing peace to what he supposes is his lover's inner turmoil.

At first, the narrator presents himself coolly enough, in composed and orderly, unhurried language. Only at the end of the poem do we learn that he has spent all night cuddling the cold corpse of the woman he has strangled! We might expect, therefore, the language at the start of the poem to reflect a crazed state of mind. Hence, retrospectively we are appalled by his calmness and composure, implying as it does his lack of moral awareness of the horror of what has done.

At first, though the poem is arranged on the page in one relentless, unbroken block, it appears to be written in quatrains. But closer inspection of the rhyme reveals a consistent pattern of five line stanzas, sometimes called cinquains. In one way, maintaining the consistent regularity of this pattern indicates the tense control the narrator exerts, over his own emotions as well as the poem's language and form. On the other hand, the five-line stanzas encode imbalance as the key structural building block of the poem. With either one or two rhyme words, a quatrain is a balanced form. A cinquain, however, has both an odd number of lines and, in Browning's version, an asymmetrical rhyme pattern in which the second rhyme dominates the first: ABABB – CDCDD – EFEFF – GHGHH and so on. It's not a great leap of the imagination to see this rhyme pattern as reflecting the uneven relationship between the two lovers.

Generally, the cinquains are neatly ordered - quite a few end with a full stop, expressing skilful alignment of sentences, syntax, metre and rhyme. The poet's skill here creates the impression of calm articulacy in the narrator. But this calm surface is a mask, a mask hiding underlying tensions, darker currents. At times the strain of maintaining appearances begins to seep through into the verse and the mask slips. The poet ensures that disturbance worms its way underneath the calm surface of lines, particularly at crucial points in the narrative. Sometimes the disturbance is quite subtle, such as in the poem's first caesura which creates a distinct pause immediately after the entrance of Porphyria. Another example would be lines in which the metre varies or which have extra syllables. At other times, the strain on the narrator to maintain an appearance of normality becomes more obvious. For example, the sentence starting with 'when voice replied' runs on for eleven, winding and excitable lines. The narrator's agitation at this point in the story is also signalled by the run of breathless 'ands' at the starts of lines. The simplest conjunction is used to link independent clauses together, suggesting there is something infantile in his excited possessiveness. This impression is enhanced by obsessive cataloguing of Porphyria's every action. Though the narrator may wish to present himself as rational and his actions as sane, the poet ensures he cannot quite disguise his jealous mania.

Blue eyes without a stain

So much for our tormented narrator. What do we learn about the poem's other main character, the murdered woman, Porphyria? Of course, we must bear in mind that everything we learn about her we hear through the tainted voice of a madman and a murderer, but nevertheless we can establish some of her key characteristics. In comparison to the static, observing narrator Porphyria is all go. We are given a kind of inventory of all Porphyria's many actions when she arrives at the cottage: she 'glided', 'shut', kneeled', 'made', 'rose', 'withdrew', 'laid', 'untied', 'let', 'sat' and, finally, but perhaps too late, 'called'. She is an active, compelling presence and every one of her movements is obsessively noted and catalogued. Immediately and symbolically, she brings warmth, energy and light to the cold, dark, miserable cottage: She 'shut the cold out and the storm'; she made the 'cheerless grate/ blaze up'.

Just as the rhyme scheme encodes the uneven relationship between the lovers, the same is signalled by Browning's symbolism. The narrator is like the cold, isolated cottage he inhabits; Porphyria is a force of light and energy. But she is also dangerous, at least in terms of her effect on her surroundings; she makes the fire 'blaze'.

The narrator describes Porphyria as 'perfectly pure and good'. She's a vivacious presence in the poem and shows devotion to her lover, leaving a bright party [the 'gay feast'], travelling through 'wind and rain' to a remote cottage to be with him. Why then does he kill her?

Inside the mind of a murderer

Good question. The answer is that he narrator is so obsessed by Porphyria that he cannot bare to share her with anyone or anything else. Hence, he refers to her 'weak' inability to break free of any ties to society: 'From pride,' she cannot 'vainer ties dissever/ And give herself' to him 'for ever.' 'Pride' and 'vainer ties' imply Porphyria may come from a higher class than a lover who resides in a lowly cottage. He she can't sever herself from society he must do this for her. And the only way he can think of to make her entirely his forever is by killing her. He also excuses himself of her murder by imagining this to be an act of mercy. By killing her he destroys the conflicts he imagines torment her.

The moment of murder is presented skilfully, and chillingly, by Browning:

'That moment she was mine, mine, fair,

Perfectly pure and good: I found

A thing to do, and all her hair

In one long yellow string I wound

Three times her little throat around,

And strangled her. No pain felt she;

I am quite sure she felt no pain.'

Repetition of the possessive pronoun conveys mania, but the narrator also realises that this delicious ecstasy of full possession will be short-lived; it is only in this 'moment' that he possesses her. The horror of what he is about to do is then accentuated by drawing attention to Porphyria's innocence and goodness, and by the fact that though he recognises these qualities in her, this will not prevent him from killing her. Porphyria's neck is also described as 'little' which suggests child-like vulnerability. 'A thing to do' is creepily, crazily euphemistic. It sounds casual and inconsequential, like this is a perfectly ordinary and sensible thing to do, but also shows the narrator veering away from naming the act of murder. Enjambment runs all these lines into each other, so that the killing happens very quickly, without any pause of hesitation. The caesura in the penultimate line has the opposite effect, cutting off the flow of the poem, stopping it dead. Flat monosyllables in the next four words convey the hollowness of the claim, a hollowness emphasised the more through being repeated in the next line.

With the murder the narrator's madness comes into full view. Deludedly, he believes he has fulfilled his lover's 'darling one wish', that, though she is now dead, she will be 'glad' that he has fulfilled her 'utmost will', by killing her. Queasily, we are given the impression that his passion for has grown stronger as a result of her ultimate passivity. Now he kisses her with a 'burning kiss', an image that recalls the 'blaze' in the grate. This is a man who has murdered an innocent woman to capture forever the moment of absolute surrender to his love. A Latin scholar, Browning used the word 'perfectly' very deliberately. A perfect thing, from its Latin root 'perfectus' meaning finished, is a finished thing, a complete thing - a dead thing. In his terms, she has been purified and preserved: now her eyes are 'without stain'. There is nowhere to go from perfect. In the crazed mind of this murderer, stilling that perfection is perfectly logical, even admirable.

"Pefectly pure and pure good"

The choice of the simile of the bee in the lines 'As a shut bud that holds a bee /I warily oped her lids' signals that, despite his protests that what he has done has been in Prophyria's interest, deep down he has some awareness of the wrong he has committed. It is as if he expects, at some stage, to be stung. Propping her 'little head' on his shoulder, he sits all evening with her cold corpse, waiting for someone to find them. And, perhaps, for God to deliver this 'sting' by punishing him.

We mentioned earlier that the though the poem's rhyme scheme reveals a pattern of cinquains it is set out on the page as one, unbroken continuous block. What difference, if any, do you think it would it make if the poem were set out in separate stanzas?

↳ More ordered, measured tone, pauses for breath

Porphyria's Lover crunched: ↳ Black shows domination and impetuousness

NIGHT – SULLEN - SPITE – VEX – BREAK – GLIDED – SHUT OUT – CHEERLESS – WAMR – ROSE – WITHDREW – SOILED – HAIR – SAT – CALLED – WAIST – BARE – YELLOW – STOOPING – SPREAD – LOVED – WEAK – STRUGGGLING – DISSEVER – FOR EVER – PASSION – FEAST – PALE – VAIN – COME – EYES – HAPPY – WORSHIPPED – SWELL – DO – MINE – GOOD – THING – WOUND – THROAT – STRANGLED – PAIN – BEE – WARILY – STAIN – UNTIGHTENED – CHEEK – BLUSHING – PROPPED – ONLY – DROOPS – LITTLE – GLAD – SCORNED – GAINED – LOVE – WISH – TOGHETHER – NIGHT – GOD.

A crunchier crunch:

RAIN – HEART – BLAZE – HAIR – BARE – WEAK – PASSION – VAIN – MINE –STRANGLED – HEAD – GOD.

NB

If you've still a taste for the macabre after reading this poem, you might want to try Browning's other great poem about fanatically possessive and murderous 'love', *My Last Duchess*. The fact that both poems feature vivacious women caught and murdered by jealous men highlights the proto-feminist aspect of Browning's poems. Like the painting by Holman Hunt below, Browning's poems were part of a rising protest against the oppression of women by patriarchal society, a protest that would grow into the suffrage movement. Although, having said that, is there anything you can find to confirm that the narrator of *Porphyria's Lover* actually is a man?

Elizabeth Barrett Browning, *Sonnet 29, I think of thee!*

A modest disguise

Elizabeth Barrett Browning's Sonnet 29, *I think of thee*, is a poem of intense and passionate yearning for an absent lover. If you've been in love and experienced how you can't seem to stop thinking about that person when they are not with you, so that your thoughts seem out-of-control and threaten to overwhelm you, then you will recognise what the poet expresses in this poem. She wrote it as a private expression of her love for the poet Robert Browning, with whom she had begun a secret courtship. The couple later married, but her father disowned her as he did not approve of her choice. It was only after they were married that Elizabeth mentioned she had written a series of sonnets about her husband while they were courting. When he read them, he thought they were the best sonnets written in English since Shakespeare's and encouraged her to publish. However, they were so personal and revealing, having never been intended for anyone other than Elizabeth Barrett Browning herself, that they were published under the title *Sonnets from the Portuguese*, in an attempt to pretend they were obscure translations of another poet, rather than intimate expressions of her own private emotions. This accounts for the intensely personal tone of *Sonnet 29*; when we write about this poem we can confidently talk about the poet's own feelings rather than those of a dramatized speaker, although inevitably there is always some act of dramatization to any poem, regardless of how closely and accurately the poet wants to express their own personality in their work.

A technical challenge

To fully appreciate Barrett Browning's art and achievement in this poem, we first need to understand something of the poetic form in which she chose to compose it - the sonnet. In the twentieth and twenty-first centuries, poets have experimented greatly with sonnets, but traditionally they tend to be love poems and have a very strict poetic structure that place a number of rules or limitations on the poet, making them challenging to write. Sonnets must have fourteen lines and tend to be written in iambic pentameter, lines of ten syllables that alternate between an unstressed and a stressed syllable, as in the opening line of *Sonnet 29* where Barrett Browning writes 'I **think** of **thee**! - my **thoughts** do **twine** and **bud**'. Sonnets also tend to follow a distinctive rhyming pattern. There are different variations of sonnets depending on how the ideas are arranged and what the rhyme scheme is, but the most common types are the Petrarchan (also known as Italian) sonnet, the Spenserian and the Shakespearean sonnet. *Sonnet 29* is written as a Petrarchan sonnet, probably the most challenging form for writers in English due to the more limited number of rhymes. Traditionally Petrarchan sonnets are divided into an octave of eight lines (rhyming abbaabba) that presents a problem, followed by a sestet of six lines which presents the solution. The rhyme scheme for the sestet can be more flexible but tends to follow cdecde or cdcdcd. The transition from the octave to the sestet where the poem shifts from a problem to a solution occurs between the eighth and ninth lines and is known as a *volta*, which means 'turn' in Italian. Barret Browning was an accomplished sonnet writer and most of her sonnets follow the rules impeccably, but what makes this poem remarkable is the way in which she deliberately breaks some of the rules of the sonnet to create particular effects and communicate specific meanings that powerfully reveal the emotions she is feeling.

My thoughts do twine and bud

Although the poem was originally only intended for Elizabeth herself, she starts the poem by addressing her future husband, Robert Browning, when she writes 'I think of thee!' The exclamation mark emphasises the excitement he makes her feel, as do the short, simple, monosyllabic words that create the impression that nothing else is important to her. The archaic pronoun 'thee' also generates a much more intimate tone than using 'you' might and appears seven times in the poem, demonstrating just how important and all-encompassing her future husband was to her. 'Thee' also suggests, particularly as Barrett Browning was a devout Christian, the religious language of the King James Bible, where it appears 2,738 times, elevating her love for Robert Browning almost into the spiritual sphere of devotional love for God himself.

However, no sooner does the poet begin to think of her love than her thoughts are interrupted by the dash in line one, which creates a pause in the rhythm, known as a caesura. The caesura again emphasises the importance of 'thee' by forcing us to dwell on this word, but it also suggests the poet is not quite in control of her thoughts as if they are taking on a life and direction of their own. This leads into the next part of the poem where Barrett Browning introduces the poem's central image: 'my thoughts do twine and bud/ About thee, as wild vines, about a tree'. Here, she uses a simile to compare her thoughts about Robert to a vine that wraps itself around the trunk of a tree as it climbs up and smothers the tree's bark. She draws once again on Biblical language, this time from *Song of Songs* in *The Old Testament*, where the female speaker in the book also compares her love to a palm tree and says 'thy stature is like to a palm tree...I will take hold of the boughs thereof: now also thy breasts shall be as clusters of the vine'. *Song of Songs* is

a celebration of sexual love and there is an equally charged, erotic dimension to Barrett Browning's poem, the verb 'twine' suggestive of the poet wrapping herself around her lover, the adjective 'wild' evocative of an uncontrolled release of passion and desire, and the image of the tree a barely disguised phallic symbol. Such details might make a prudish reader blush even today; imagine, then, how shocking the poem's sentiments might have been to a Victorian reader, particularly so as the writer of this sensual, erotic material is, of course, female.

However, while she delights in her love, the problem for the poet is that her thoughts and emotions seem to be growing out-of-control, something she cleverly evokes through the use of enjambment. Her thoughts in line one, for example, spill over into line two. The caesuras after 'thee' and 'vines' in line two also suggest the sudden growth of ideas or change of direction, as if her thoughts are wrapping themselves around the poem like the vines around the tree. Irrepressible growth is also evoked through the way the simile comparing her thoughts to a vine and the man she loves to a tree evolves into an extended metaphor - also known as a conceit - that weaves itself throughout the whole poem. The central problem that the octave presents is that the poet's overpowering thoughts for this man are clouding and obscuring the man himself, so that she can no longer see him clearly. He becomes more and more submerged under her thoughts, in the same way a vine might grow up and around a tree, hiding its bark and true form. As she says in the next two lines, 'and soon there's nought to see/ Except the straggling green which hides the wood'. Here, the verb 'straggling' gives a strong sense of the way her thoughts have become unkempt and overgrown. We can also almost hear the word 'strangling', which is what a vine eventually does to a tree if left unchecked, implying that her thoughts risk completing destroying the true image of the man himself. But as she determines in line six, 'I will not have my thoughts instead of thee'. For the solution to her problem, we now need to turn to the sonnet's sestet.

Rustle thy boughs

In a traditional Petrarchan sonnet, the volta, which indicates the turn of thought towards a solution, normally happens between the eighth and ninth lines. In *Sonnet 29*, however, it occurs earlier in lines 7-8 where the poet pleads with her love to 'Rather, instantly/ Renew thy presence'. The simple solution to the poet's problem of her out-of-control longing for her love is for him to appear and no longer be absent. Barrett Browning deliberately places the volta earlier than it should do in a sonnet to express her impatience to see her love, the overwhelming love she feels for him causing her to throw aside the normal rules and strictures of traditional sonnet writing. This sense of urgency and excitement is also captured in the enjambment at the end of the seventh line, which hastens the reader onto the next line without time for pause or hesitation. Her insistence that he comes to her immediately to bridge their absence is further accentuated through the use of imperative verbs throughout this section, such as the command in line nine to 'Rustle thy boughs and set thy trunk all bare'. She also reverses the rhythm of the poem at the start of this line by using a trochee (a stressed syllable followed by an unstressed, as in 'Rustle') rather than an iamb (an unstressed syllable followed by a stressed, as in 'Renew' in the previous line). This reversal emphasises the force of the poet's command to her love but also the reversal of her thoughts overpowering the image of her love. By appearing to her and revealing his true self, rather than the distorted version her thoughts have created, she commands the virile tree to shake free of the vine that has enshrouded and cloaked it.

Barrett Browning also uses sibilance to great effect in this section. Examples include lines eight and nine, in which words such as 'presence', 'as', 'strong', 'should', 'Rustle', 'boughs' and 'set', evoke the sound of rustling leaves as the tree breaks free of the vines. Enjambment is again used to striking effect, as when she commands her love to 'let these bands of greenery which insphere thee/ Drop heavily down', forcing the reader to drop down the lines as the vine leaves fall from the tree. The alliteration of the plosive 'd' sounds in

'Drop heavily down' further emphasises the forcefulness with which the tree shakes itself free, as does the violence of the verbs 'burst' and 'shattered' later in the line. The caesura in the middle of this line after 'down' creates a momentary pause, long enough to build up the energy that reaches a triumphant climax of 'burst, shattered, everywhere!', which reaches its crescendo by building up a one, two and then three syllable word, followed by the emphatic exclamation.

This deep joy

The poem's final sentence which runs across the last three lines envisages an end to the lovers' separation. The excitement the poet feels and 'the deep joy to see and hear thee', as she imagines her love's presence, is captured in the simple, monosyllabic words, the line's extra eleventh syllable, as well as the enjambment that flows seamlessly onto the penultimate line. Now that her thoughts no longer obscure her love from view, she can see him clearly and 'breathe within thy shadow a new air' in language that again echoes the female lover of Song of Songs who says of her love, 'I sat down under his shadow with great delight, and his fruit was sweet to my taste'. The poem's final line enacts a full reversal of the poem's opening; where the poet began by acknowledging 'I think of thee', now she reveals 'I do not think of thee'. This is not because he has become unimportant to her - far from it! Rather now, in his imagined presence, the poet states 'I am too near to thee'. Her thoughts about her love have now been replaced by something far better - the man himself. This is the seventh time the word 'thee' occurs in the poem, a number which in the Bible symbolizes completeness and perfection. The poet also draws attention to this word by making it the eleventh syllable of a line we would expect to end after ten, while also breaking the rhyming pattern of the sestet by using repetition of 'thee' at the end of lines ten, twelve and fourteen rather than rhymed words. Barrett Browning seems to be deliberately breaking the rules of the sonnet writing to suggest that perfection is not to be found in poetry, but rather in her lover, and not even the age-old rules and structures of that most traditional of love poems - the sonnet -can contain and constrain her powerful and joyful love for him.

Sonnet 29 crunched:

THEE – VINES – NOUGHT – STRAGGLING – O – INSTEAD – DEARER – TREE – BARE – BANDS – SHATTERED – JOY – BREATHE – NEAR

Thomas Hardy, *Neutral Tones*

Long, cold shadows

How do we look back on lost love, on relationships we thought were going to endure but where love did not last the test of time? Are such experiences consigned to the ash heap of history, never to be thought of again, or does something about them linger in our imagination and haunt our present? Hardy's poetry is preoccupied with ghosts, sometimes literal, but more often metaphorical spectres of the past that disturb and oppress the troubled memories of his poems' speakers. In *Neutral Tones* we see how a failed relationship casts its long and cold shadow across the narrator's subsequent life like a stone dropped into the centre of a pond whose ripple travels out to the water's far edges.

Titles are nearly always significant signposts for interpreting poems and the title of this poem is no exception. On one level, a 'neutral tone' refers to any of the chromatic colours—white, black or grey—that, scientifically speaking, are not actually colours due to their lack of hue. Hardy's poem is drained of colour, evident in the 'white' sun and 'gray' leaves. The poet even puns on 'ash' tree, which connotes the grey ash left from a fire that has burned itself out - a fitting symbol for the end of love. The lack of colour, as well as the wintry setting, implies a cold and bitter atmosphere as well as the absence of life and joy caused by the end of the relationship. However, on another level, the title could also refer to a neutral tone of voice, one characterized by the absence of any strong emotion or partial and biased opinion. While the speaker does strive to create a cool and emotionally detached tone that focuses on observation and retrospective reflection of 'lessons that love deceives' without seeking to apportion blame or dissect the relationship, we might want to question the degree to  which he is successful at exorcising strong emotional undercurrents from the poem.

One way in which we can detect the return of repressed emotions in the poem is through its formal structure. While Hardy did not write in the free verse which characterized many of the Modernist poets of the early twentieth century, he was a master experimenter within traditional metrical and stanzaic forms, which is why today he is recognized as the forerunner of modern poetry. While the first three lines of each stanza in *Neutral Tones* follows a fairly regular rhythm of four feet that consist of either an unstressed syllable followed by a stressed (iamb) or two unstressed syllables followed by a stressed (anapaest), such as 'We <u>stood</u> I by a <u>pond</u> I that <u>win</u> I ter <u>day</u>', the final line of each stanza disrupts the pattern and rhythm by reducing the line to just three feet, as in 'They had fallen I from an ash I and were gray'. The effect is to create an absence, the disappointment of something expected but not realized and an inarticulate longing for something unfulfilled. The rhythm falters and stumbles on the fourth line as emotional confusion rises to the poem's surface.

Loss, pain, inertia and hopelessness are also subtly inscribed within the poem's *abba* rhyme scheme ('day...God...sod...gray'). It is a pattern that suggests the failure to move forwards, a stagnation which returns to its point of origin. For Hardy's contemporary readers, this scheme was synonymous with Tennyson's monumental elegy for lost love, *In Memoriam*, which immortalized the lines 'Tis better to have loved and lost/ Than never to have loved at all'. Hardy rewrites Tennyson's elegy in lyric form. But, whereas Tennyson searched for meaning and consolation when love died, Hardy's poem focuses on emptiness, disappointment and the absence of meaning.

The final stanza accentuates the rhyme scheme's sense of inexorable entrapment and things not moving forward. Although we finally move from the past memory of the broken relationship in the first three stanzas to the reflective present of the fourth stanza, the recurring imagery of the tree and the pond, the 'God curst sun' and 'grayish leaves' returns us straight back to the first stanza in an infinite loop we cannot break out of. The use of polysyndeton and anaphora in the repeated use of 'And' at the start of sentences are further structural techniques emphasising the desire to move forward and break free coupled with the monotonous failure to do so.

Chidden of God

Another striking feature of the poem is the repeated diction and imagery of death that permeates its lines. As well as the winter-time setting, the decaying leaves and the apocalyptic white sun, the 'starving sod' of the first stanza personifies the earth as a victim of famine and drought, the alliterative sibilance creating a harsh and even sinister effect. Often in poetry water serves as a symbol of life and vitality, but the pond setting of this poem suggests that life has stagnated and no longer flows anywhere. In Arthurian legend, the bareness of the land indicated a curse upon it as a result of an ineffectual and powerless king. Hardy's narrator is equally powerless and the undertones of a universe cosmically blighted and cursed is made explicit in references in the first and fourth stanza to the sun 'chidden of God'. The speaker of the poem exists in a universe that God has cursed by absenting himself, leaving an existence of suffering without meaning or purpose.

However, although the poem takes us to the frontiers of metaphysical speculation, this is not the main preoccupation of the poem. Rather, at the centre of the poem lies the memory of the failed relationship and, in particular, the image of the lover's face that haunts the speaker in the middle two stanzas. Eyes and lips are common images in love poetry but here, Hardy subverts their associations by making them accusatory of weariness and disillusion as with the 'eyes that rove/ Over tedious riddles' and the 'grin of bitterness'. In particular, the verb 'rove' suggests eyes that are now interested in something or someone else other. Here, the undercurrent of feeling which the title of the poem denies once again resurfaces.

The death imagery is also continued when the speaker recalls how 'The smile on your mouth was the deadest thing/ Alive enough to have strength to die.'

This strange and oxymoronic description, where the superlative 'deadest' relates to something alive enough to die, suggests the lover's insincerity, but also the speaker's confused and hurt state of mind. The 'ominous bird' further indicates the expectation and portent of something dreadful to come

and we realise this is the moment the speaker comprehends that love is not everlasting, something which will colour all future relationships. The alliterative 'wrings with wrongs' not only creates the sound of an agonized and tormented fissure in the poem, but also puns on the word 'ring' which ironically suggests a wedding ring- that symbol of immortalized love - as well as a circle in which the speaker has become ensnared; he cannot escape from the repercussions and implication of this first realization. Where this feeling cannot be articulated, it is heard through the painful sounds of the poem, such as the 'oh' that rises from the assonantal 'rove' and 'Over' and the rhyme of 'ago' and 'fro' in the second stanza, or the tormented 'ee' sounds of the final stanza in 'keen', 'deceives', 'tree' and 'leaves'. 'Keen' also means sharp which again reveals the sense of pain that underlies the poem. Throughout the poem then, where the neutral tones of the surface suggest detachment and cool contemplation, the true, painful and inexpressible feelings frequently rise from the depths to be detected in the poem's structures, textures and sounds.

Neutral Tones crunched:

WINTER – WHITE – STARVING – ASH – EYES – TEDIOUS – WORDS – LOST – DEADEST – ENOUGH – BITTERNESS – OMINOUS – DECEIVES – WRONG – CURST – GREYISH

Maura Dooley, *Letters From Yorkshire*

First lapwings

It's an unusual opening. The first clause, 'In February', tells us nothing about the speaker of the poem, nor its subject, nor does it give us any indication of tense, and yet it is enormously evocative. In conjunction with the poem's title, it stirs images of icy winter mist drifting over the moors in the early morning light. The rest of the first line gives us a subject, with 'his garden' suggesting a 'he' at the centre of the poem. Noticeably, later in the poem the gap between the writer and this 'he' closes as the 'he' becomes a more intimate 'you', but for now 'he' is viewed as from a distance. Two present continuous verbs, 'digging' and 'planting', evade any attempt to securely place the poem in a timeframe. The aspirant plosives of 'planting potatoes' and the hard 'g' sounds of 'digging his garden' create an earthy phonological texture, immediately rooting the opening of the poem in the natural world that will be a fundamental theme throughout. But it's also an unusual

69

opening in that the first line is so long, the longest line in the entire poem, by some way, with 15 syllables – if you count 'February' as four – at least two syllables longer than any of the others. Despite such a rambling length, the line's structure remains relatively intact. Its five main stressed syllables makes it a very loose pentameter, a metre that ticks through most of the rest of the poem.

The rest of the first stanza gives us a clear sense of timing. 'He saw the first lapwings return' indicates the past tense, during which he was 'digging his

garden' and 'planting potatoes'. The importance of time and the seasons becomes clearer – not only does the poem open with the setting 'in February', but the return of 'the first lapwings' is a significant moment, a milestone that triggers the action of the poem.

Dooley chooses not to capitalise the first letter of the first word of each line; a slightly unusual formatting choice in poetry. The effect is to give a greater sense of flow from line to line, as the beginning of each new line feels less like a definitive new beginning and more like a continuation of what came before. This is put to particularly good use in this poem, as the sense of each phrase comes more from its punctuation and sentence divides, and less from the line breaks. So when 'he saw the first lapwings return and came / indoors to write to me', the new line doesn't stand out; the lowercase letter on 'indoors' leads the reader to flow seamlessly into the next line.

As the male figure in the poem comes inside, the poem shifts. Whereas before, the focus had been on the natural world, on 'digging', 'potatoes', and 'lapwings', the narrative switches to 'knuckles', writing, and the 'warmth'. The personification of 'his knuckles singing / as they reddened in the warmth' further shifts the focus. The fourth line is also shorter, with only three major stresses and seven syllables, which leaves a gulf after the word 'warmth', as if the warmth itself expands and settles across the line, like a deep sigh on sinking into a comfortable sofa.

The tone of the poem as a whole is comfortably informal, and the fifth perhaps the most informal. 'It's not romance, simply how things are' is the language of colloquial conversation. There is no conjunction joining the two clauses, where a 'but' might have been expected. The elision of 'it' and 'is' into the informal 'it's' is a further signal, and 'things' – with its characteristic friendly vagueness – shows this is a poem in an informal register. The short, simple sentence is almost a paraphrase of what the male subject of the poem might say; a common catchphrase remembered by the poem's speaker, or a modest protest to counter the speaker's fanciful imagination.

Me & you

With the pronoun 'you' at the beginning of the sixth line, the poem's perspective shifts again. For the first time we get a sense of the poem's speaker, an 'I' that can point at somebody else and identify a 'you'. The contrast is clearly evoked between 'you out there, in the cold, seeing the seasons / turning, me with my heartful of headlines / feeding words onto a blank screen'. The difference the speaker presents between these two worlds is huge. 'The cold' is intended to contrast clearly with the earlier 'warmth' that reddened his knuckles earlier in the poem, and with the warm air that the alliteration of 'heartful of headlines' creates. The verbs, too, are different. 'Seeing' and 'turning' depict a dignified kind of spectatorship – watching the grand arc of life and the year unfold in front of you, whilst 'feeding' evokes the practical needs of life, the day-to-day, eat-and-drink, as much as it hints at the vulgar implications of hunger, lust, devouring, and appetite. The flow of the two worlds is different, too. In his perspective, the world comes to him; he sees it, absorbs it, it turns and he admires it. The world of the speaker is 'a blank screen' – the harsh 'k' sounds of 'blank' and 'screen' jar on the voice – which has to be actively fed in order for it to offer anything at all.

The speaker finishes the third stanza with a direct, perhaps even confrontational question – 'Is your life more real because you dig and sow?'

The heaviest of the stresses in this line fall on monosyllabic words; 'life', 'real', 'dig', and 'sow', giving it a rugged, down-to-earth quality. The world of the male subject, of the outdoors, of Yorkshire, is a solid, grounded world of simple monosyllabic words. But it's a world that, to the poet, seems as much a fabrication as a firm reality. The fourth stanza's opening 'you' is again a kind of awakening, and could be interpreted as sounding accusatory, even aggressive. The simple language of the conjecture 'you wouldn't say so' speaks honestly and plainly, and couples with the workaday tasks of 'breaking ice on a waterbutt' (which is a kind of outdoor water tank that looks like a bin) and 'clearing a path through snow'.

A caesura provides a clear break before the speaker defends her vision of the 'real' idyll of the natural Yorkshire life with an assertive 'still'. The alliteration of the 'word of that other world' creates worlds of words of its own, spinning a web of writing and communication that is capable of 'pouring air and light into an envelope'. This is a strikingly lyrical metaphor that might suggest the writing of a poem. Except that here, it seems, it is the addressee who is doing the 'pouring'. In this sense, the poem implies the apparent divide between the two worlds might be bridgeable or, indeed merely a false perception. At first the image may seem liberating and beautiful; capturing the beauty of the space and stillness in the *Letters From Yorkshire* through language and compressing it into the tight space of an envelope. But it is at the same time a metaphor that feels claustrophobic – an envelope has no air and light in it, it has no space for air and no way of letting in light, so 'pouring air and light into an envelope' will only, eventually, result in that air and light being lost, dissipating. Ultimately the image is melancholy; distance still separates the speaker of the poem from her subject, his natural and earthy world.

Across the icy miles

The poem's ending reinforces that melancholy distance between the speaker and the poem's subject. The mundanity of 'watching the same news in different houses' – the more active verb 'seeing' from earlier in the poem replaced with the passive 'watching' – comes as a stark contrast to the yearning implied in 'our souls tap out messages across the icy miles'. The word 'soul' is important. It fits neither in the down-to-earth natural world of 'digging', 'potatoes', 'seasons', and 'the cold', nor in the internal world of people and things, of 'heartful of headlines', the 'blank screen', and the 'knuckles singing / as they reddened in the warmth'. The two 'souls' seem to

73

cross that boundary, the central divide that runs like a thread through the poem, and occupy a middle ground. The verb phrase 'tap out messages' seems unlike any we've read so far. 'Tap' has a physicality and a real-world noisiness to it, but also is used to refer to the silent tapping of fingers on touch-screen phones in a technologically-driven world increasingly separate from the natural one. And where the title of the poem speaks of 'letters', and the real interactions of two people with simple rhetorical questions and emphatic denials, the ending offers only 'messages'. Are these secret codes; ways of hinting at the unspeakable yearnings and longings that separate the two figures in the  poem 'across the icy miles'? Or are these on a less profound level simply the messages of life in the digital age – the texts and emails we send in a desperate attempt to keep up?

Dooley's poem contrasts mundanity and profundity, the man-made world versus the natural world, in depicting the distance, separation, and yearning between two individuals whose exact relationship is unknown. Are they friends, family members, or even – perhaps – lovers? The poem offers no clear guides as to what kind of interaction they have, but is told in an informal register with an atmosphere that is melancholic and yearning, hinting at some deeper connection that has been lost, or has been rendered difficult by 'the icy miles'. The lack of a clear rhyme scheme emphasises that distance, with internal rhymes within and between lines offering distant echoes of familiarity outside of the comforting chimes of the line-ending rhymes we're used to reading. 'Word' and 'world' echo each other, while 'light' and 'night' harmonise in their opposition; 'houses' and 'messages' seem suggestive of each other, as do 'news' and 'miles'. Extensive use of the present continuous tense gives a feeling of happening, like the seasons constantly in flow for the male subject, or the constant hunger of the 'blank screen' that constantly requires 'feeding' for the speaker. Dooley sets out the 'romance' of *Letters From Yorkshire*, with its images of natural beauty, working the land, and workaday diligence, but ultimately distorts the image in distance and melancholy. Where the writerly speaker of the poem craves the feeling of closeness through the *Letters From Yorkshire*, she gets merely 'texts' in front of the television, more conscious than ever of the apparent gulf 'across the icy miles'.

Same news in different houses

Or is it possible to read this last image and, indeed, the whole poem in a more positive light? That, for instance, despite the distances between them there is a deep, enduring communion between the two characters' souls. Perhaps. Read the above line again. Your interpretation of the poem may Just hinge on which of the two adjectives, 'same' and 'different' you choose to emphasise.

Letters from Yorkshire crunched:

DIGGING – HE – ME – WARMTH – ROMANCE – YOU – HEADLINE – BLANK – REAL – ICE – SNOW – OTHER – POURING – DIFFERENT - SOULS

Charlotte Mew, *The Farmer's Bride*

Sometimes it appears that poets live more extraordinary lives than the rest of us. Romantic poets, for instance, such as Byron and Shelley burnt brightly and died young. Witness too the startling biographical facts of Charlotte Mew's tragic life: Born in 1869, the eldest of seven children into a middle-class London family, Charlotte was still a child when three of her siblings died. A little later a brother and a sister were committed to asylums where they spent their entire lives. Charlotte lived with her mother and her remaining sister, Anne, for the rest of their lives, making a pact with Anne not to ever marry or have children for fear of passing on the family's history of mental illness on to another generation. After Anne's death, Charlotte sunk into depression and only a year later the poet died in a sanatorium through taking her own life in 1928. All rather distressingly grim. Yet, in her own peculiar, intense way, Charlotte also burned brightly too and was considered by some important people to be one of the foremost female poets of her age.

Set in the recent past, *The Farmer's Bride* is a dramatic monologue, written in the rustic voice of a farmer. Considering that the poem's overt subject is the unnamed wife we might wonder why Mew chose not to use her as the narrator. Clearly this decision serves to emphasise the wife's lack of voice and agency in her life; just as she is defined by her relationship to a man, she is a 'wife', she also is not able to tell her own story.

What impression do we form of the farmer?

In his rugged, earthy vernacular, the farmer tells his story in a straightforward, forthright sort of way and assumes that the reader will share a similar view of the affair. Mew uses a number of non-standard phrases to create the farmer's voice: 'More's to do'; 'when us was wed'; ''tradn't a woman'; 'runned away'; 'her be'; 'wadn't' and so forth. A practical man-of-the-land, he is business-like and unromantic about getting married. He doesn't have time, for instance, to waste 'woo'ing a wife, i.e. courting and getting to know her; he simply chose what seemed to him a suitable seeming maid. In the same way he might have chosen the right piece of agricultural machinery for a particular task. He seems surprised that his young wife runs away and tells of how they 'chased her', brought her back and locked her up 'fast', a word that suggests both 'quickly and

'securely'. Though he is capable of articulacy, such as the poignant simile of her smile going out 'like the shut of a winter's day', predominantly his voice is rugged and direct and the details of the story are told briskly, without any real emotion or fuss. After her failed escape, the wife is put to work and she

77

does her domestic tasks, he tells us, 'as well as most'. In the penultimate stanza, the farmer expresses his desire for a child and how this desire has been frustrated by a lack of contact with his wife. For the first time in the last stanza we hear him express some sympathy for her plight, referring to her as the 'poor maid'.

The farmer emerges from his own story as a somewhat gruff, no-nonsense, insensitive, but fundamentally ordinary man. He doesn't appear to be intentionally mean or cruel. Nor does he take any sadistic pleasure from his wife's obvious distress. He's not then, a monster or a villain; he's not out-and-out bad, at least in his own mind. But, in some ways, doesn't this just make the situation worse? The fact that his attitudes are so ordinary; the fact that such an ordinary man could treat his wife so monstrously; the fact and that he is not even conscious that what he is doing is monstrous. Furthermore, the farmer expresses no contrition, regret or remorse about his treatment of a woman he is supposed to love. In fact, he presents her behaviour as if it is unreasonable and inexplicable. And, while that adjective 'poor' might have implied he had at least some pity for his wife this is more than counterbalanced by the lustful way the poem ends with his obsessing over the 'soft young down' of her body, her brown eyes and hair. The farmer may not be aware that his treatment of his wife is brutish, unjust and callous, but Mew ensures that the reader arrives firmly at this opinion. This ironic gap that opens up between how the narrator thinks he is presenting himself and how the reader reads him is essential to all good dramatic monologues. Mew gives us enough information to reconstruct for ourselves a rather different version of the narrative, focused on the brutal injustice of the wife's experience and on her feelings. In effect, as readers, we are positioned by Mew as the wife and construct her story ourselves.

A young larch tree

From her husband's description of their truncated or non-existent 'courtship' the wife was very young and had absolutely no choice other than to be  married to him. NO mention is made of her consent to marriage or of the option of her rejecting his suit. She is picked off the peg by her husband like an object he takes a fancy to and has use of. Her feelings about an event that will shape the course of her life are entirely irrelevant. In addition to the complete absence of romance or love, the idea that she ought to have any choice in the matter of marriage does not even cross her husband's consciousness, let alone his conscience. Instead, he matter-of-factly informs us that soon after the wedding she 'turned afraid'. What made her afraid? What was she frightened of? 'Of love and me' her husband unashamedly tells us. As at the end of the poem, we understand that this narrator has only the most rudimentary understanding of love and relationships. He does, however, experience lust. Hence, we infer that what he means by 'love' here is actually sex. In the light of the fact that the wife was a 'maid', which suggests her virginity, that she is so 'young', an adjective repeated three times for emphasis in the poem, considering too that she had no say in her marriage and bearing in mind that her husband is so crudely lacking in emotional empathy, we are likely to appreciate why she was so scared by, and resistant to, his sexual advances. In this context, the reference to the terror in her eye and her shrinking away when any one of the local men 'comes within reach' takes on a more disturbing, even sinister dimension. As does the detail that 'tis but a stair' that separates her from her husband's lustful yearnings.

Frightened by her husband, the girl runs away into the night and the darkness. Though she puts up a fight [they catch her 'at last'], she is hunted down like an animal, trapped and forcibly returned 'home'. Her animalistic terror is made tangible: 'All in a shiver and a scare we caught her'. At this point she is effectively imprisoned, [we} 'turned the key upon her'. That plural pronoun indicates that the husband did not act alone; if his behaviour is ordinary, yet monstrous, it seems sanctioned and supported by the people around him. Nobody protests or speaks up for the girl or considers she might have any rights. Indeed, this raises the issue of other agents in the poem, or rather how key agents have gone missing. No mention is made at all of the girl's mother or father. They appear to be completely insignificant; certainly they provide no protection or care for their child in the way we might hope and expect. Effectively, it seems, she is an orphan. No mention is made either of siblings, so she seems entirely alone and at the mercy of a world in which she has no rights.

The young wife finds some comfort communing with nature and she is, of course, compared in several similes to animals and plants. In particular, twice she reminds her husband of young hare; chased, she runs 'like a hare' and she is also 'shy as a leveret'. Her timidity reminds him of a 'mouse'. Later her young, 'slight' frame is compared to a 'young larch tree' and she's described as being 'sweet' as 'wild violets'. All these images objectify and dehumanise her, presenting her as a small, vulnerable thing. Her wildness, youth [is she much more than a child?] and kinship with nature imply her utter unsuitability for the role of domestic drudge and dutiful, child-bearing wife. None of the images reveal of her inner world, her thoughts, feelings or her true character.

Because, even after three years of marriage, this is of little or no interest to her husband.

Domination and control

The farmer's wife is little more than a slave; she has no control over or agency in her life or even the telling of her life. If the poem is set before the Married Women's Property acts of the 1870s, legally she would also be the property of her husband and not able to have any income of her own. Before these acts, her chances of securing a divorce would have been infinitesimally small. However, there is a sense in which her 'wildness' remains ungoverned and unknowable to her husband, an inner core of her being he is unable to access or control. Perhaps the form of Mew's poem also subtly encodes resistance to domination into its fabric and framework.

The first stanza lays down a complex rhyme scheme, mostly of paired rhymes. However, one rhyme 'day', 'fay', 'away' bucks this pattern. The second stanza deviates from the rhyme pattern of the first, encoding change into the structure of the poem. However, in this stanza the couplet becomes dominant, reflecting the control the farmer asserts over his wife. The initial holding pattern of paired rhyme comes under further strain in the third stanza, with the uneven pattern of triplet rhymes gaining the upper hand over paired rhymes. By the fourth stanza the whole original pattern has fallen away to be replaced by a quatrain with a desperately insistent quadruple rhyme building egocentrically to the pronoun 'me'. The fifth stanza reasserts more regularity, though with eight and a different rhyme scheme it is still a variation on the opening pattern. The poem concludes with another truncated stanza, with another different number of lines, this time five, and the final rhyme of the poem is a triplet, not a pair. If the shifting, restless rhyme scheme may signal resistance to the narrator's control, the utterly consistent use of masculine rhymes throughout the whole poem suggests his grip is still pretty firm.

The Farmer's Bride crushed:

MAID – YOUNG – WOO – AFRAID – LOVE – WINTER'S – OUT – FRIGHTENED – RUNNED – SHEEP – PROPERTY – WADN'T – STARE – SEVEN-ACRE – CHASED – LANTERNS – SCARE – CAUGHT – KEY – WORK – MOUSE – ENOUGH – BIRDS – AWAY – BESEECH – REACH – WOMEN – CHILDREN – SPEAK – LEVERET – SLIGHT – WILD – ME – SHORTEN – GREY – FALLS – LIE – BLACK – REDDEN – CHRISTMAS – OTHER – ATTIC – ALONE – GOD – DOWN – FAIR

We never hear the voice of this oppressed young woman. Even when she protests against her cruel treatment only her eyes 'speak'. Effectively she is silenced and her voice lost. Excavate her voice and write her version of events. Attempt either the standard option of writing a letter or take the more ambitious challenge of writing a dramatic monologue in her voice.

Cecil Day Lewis, *Walking Away*

Former member of the Communist party, Professor of Poetry at Oxford University, polished civil servant, poet laureate and father of the celebrated actor Daniel, Cecil Day Lewis lived, it seems, a full life. On the surface, in public, Day Lewis must also have seemed a confident, assured character. However his poem, *Walking Away*, suggests a different, more troubled, more private side to his character, as he gnaws at a memory he cannot seem to resolve.

Drifting away

The first stanza of this poem is riddled with a sense of uncertainty. The declarative 'it is eighteen years ago' is immediately offset with the qualifier of 'almost to the day', then in turn hazed by the attempt to remember the specifics of the day – 'a sunny day with leaves just turning'. Almost every line in the stanza is broken by a heavy caesura – the comma in the first line adds to the feeling of grasping at some half-forgotten memory, while the dash at the end of the line casts the reader adrift. The poem's movement is uncertain and hesitant. A second dash that closes the subordinate clause, in the third line, is a jarring jump in sense, from 'the touch-lines new-ruled' to, finally, the sentence's resolution, its subject - 'since I watched you play'. Two commas either side of 'then' in the fourth line add further heavy breaks; long pauses that slow down the words as they pass, halting the flow of the sense, stopping and starting. The final line of the stanza also has a caesura. The comma after 'wrenched from orbit' works with enjambment into the second stanza to leave the whole first stanza feeling disjointed, uncertain, incomplete. The anxiety of the poem's speaker is clear.

While the first stanza sets up a basic pentameter, the last line falls short, with only four main stressed syllables, despite having a standard total of ten syllables in the line. The line, essentially, goes 'drifting away' into the next stanza, like a forgotten thought trailing off into the ether. It flows into the next stanza, and the 'scatter of boys', which is followed by another heavy caesura in the full stop. The hesitant tread and anxious mood continue into the second stanza, with the present continuous tense of 'drifting' and 'walking' creating a sense of permanent movement, of transience, change and things shifting. The 'touch-lines new-rules', two compound nouns with

their awkward, clunky hyphens, represent not just the painted lines on the pitch, but a revision of the boundaries and demarcations of the relationship described in the poem, and the 'satellite / wrenched from its orbit' is not just a technical problem, but a painful emotion; the power of 'wrenched' as a verb is phonological as much as emotive.

The anxiety the speaker of the poem clearly sees in the subject – we assume it's his son – 'walking away from me towards the school', growing up and growing apart from him, is clear in the form. The line lengths in the second stanza shift nervously; four main stressed syllables in the first line, but then five in the second, six in the third, and four in the final two lines. The heavy stresses on 'a half-fledged thing set free', where the three final monosyllabic words all seem to demand emphasis, creates a conflict. So many heavy stresses in quick succession certainly don't sound particularly free, and the image of a bird that isn't yet built enough to fly on its own – which is what 'fledged' means – is an anxiety-inducing one. Not to mention the fact that the father calls his son a 'thing'.

The caesuras of the first stanza reappear in the second. The gulf before 'I can see' is a pause before the long phrase that continues uninterrupted until the fourth line, where 'into a wilderness' drifts off into a sound wilderness with the comma and caesura before 'the gait of one / who finds no path where the path should be'. The ambiguity of 'gait', which could sound like 'gate', is an important uncertainty, as if the subject is embarking on a journey through the gate and down the path, only there is no path, and beyond the gate is only 'a wilderness'. The twee, axiomatic-sounding final line of the stanza only unsettles further; 'who finds no path where the path should be', with its chiming repetition of the 'path' that cannot be found, echoes the sing-song banality of nursery rhymes, of maxims lectured to children to encourage them not to go wandering into the woods.

A winged seed

The directness of the 'I' and 'you' pronouns, with the implication of interaction between the speaker and the subject, slip out of reach in the third stanza as the speaker's thoughts overcome him. 'You' becomes 'that hesitant figure', while 'I' moves from direct observation, as in 'I can see', to being more reflective and philosophical, as in 'I never quite grasp'.

The natural images used throughout the poem should, in theory, serve to support the idea that as a child grows older, it makes sense that they leave the nest and grow out of the homestead, setting off in search of their own lives and their independence. But the way Day Lewis employs these natural metaphors says the opposite. The 'half-fledged thing' that is 'set free' goes before its time; unready for the  challenges of the world outside, with its wings not yet fully grown for flight. The 'winged seed loosened from its parent stem' so as to plant a new tree or flower in some other clime, is likened to the figure 'eddying away'. To 'eddy' is to move in a circular way, like smoke churning around a chimney in a billowing ring, never quite escaping. So, to describe the 'winged seed' as 'eddying away' from its parent stem seems strange; it has detached itself from the parent only to lap haplessly around, never detaching itself far enough away to forge a definitive new path, but keeping a distance that makes its absence tangible.

It is in this third stanza that the speaker's underlying uncertainty and anxiety comes to the surface. He mentions 'something I never quite grasp to convey / About nature's give-and-take', the pedantic and circumlocutory phrasing of that third line showing an anxiety, a skirting-around the issue. After the clunking caesura of the dash between 'give-and-take' and 'the small', a sense of self-editing further exacerbates the feeling of revision. 'The small', revised to 'the scorching / Ordeals' implies a fumbling desperately through the toolbox of language in search of something adequate to the feeling of being bereft at the apparent loss of a child. The enjambment of 'Ordeals', hanging as it does disjointed from the adjective with which it is paired, sharpens the cleaving. If the natural metaphors used in the poem convey an uncertainty about the due processes of a child's growth and separation from its parents, the metaphor of the 'irresolute clay' – 'irresolute' meaning uncertain or hesitant – cooked in the kiln of 'the scorching / Ordeals' is the rude awakening from that anxiety.

The fourth and final stanza of the poem sits in a different register. More formal, inward-looking, and contemplative, the lines convey how the speak reflects on his own experiences and considers what might be learned from the experience. The first two lines are both broken up by caesuras, between 'partings' and 'but none', and between 'my mind still' and 'Perhaps'. The effect of this is to split the first two lines into three main units of sense. 'I have had worse partings' and 'Perhaps it is roughly' function separately as short phrases, while 'but none that so / Gnaws at my mind still' is the anchor of the opening of the final stanza, its enjambment breaking down the barriers of the line boundaries, blurring those 'touch-lines new-ruled' from earlier and contributing to the atmosphere of uncertainty and anxiety.

Scorching ordeals

The introduction of 'God' in the third line of the final stanza complicates things. Are we then supposed to take the entire poem as an extended metaphor for God's relationship with Jesus as he took human form on earth, or even for God's detachment from the world's affairs after he created it, a theological belief called Deism that thinks God created the world and then had no part in it. Regardless of its significance, it serves to raise the register of the final stanza, and render the closing maxim – delivered after the gaping expanse of the dash at the end of a line in line 18 – all the more profound.

But even having arrived at a definitive maxim to conclude the poem, the speaker still hasn't abated his earlier nervous uncertainty. The final two lines of the poem both contain four stressed syllables, one fewer than the structure of pentameter that has been the rough foundation of the rest of the poem. It is almost as if the poem itself is 'letting go' of its syllables, watching them drift off. But it also makes it feel even more hesitant. Where the voice has been reading with five strong syllables in each line, reading four feels, at least subconsciously, more timid, tip-toeing, uncertain, particularly as the penultimate line still has 11 syllables altogether, while the last line has only nine.

The switch from the penultimate to the last line is important, too. Whereas  'selfhood begins with a walking away', love is proved, apparently, in 'the letting go'. 'A' becomes 'the'; the indefinite article transforms into the definite article. While the impression is that the determination becomes more sure – the vaguer indefinite article hardens into the definite, there's something else going on too. In a poem that habitually qualifies and checks itself – from the 'almost to the day' timidity of memory to the 'something I never quite grasp to convey' of literally clutching at sense and meaning – a more definitive conclusion would be required for us to fully believe the speaker has arrived at contentment with the situation. Instead, the faintest flicker of a shadow of a doubt creeps in, even if only through the minutiae of definite and indefinite articles.

Walking Away is a poem about separation, and the ache, anxiety, and uncertainty that this can cause. And the guilt of making, perhaps, bad decisions one cannot undo. The guilt perhaps of feeling the poet was a poor father. Certainly, parental love is shown to be a deeply troublesome, worrying experience. The poem's speaker constantly questions himself and his ability (or inability), and the poem's subject never quite proves themselves (the gender is unclear) ready or competent enough to strike out independently. The poem's form compounds this. The abaca rhyme scheme sounds like a distant  chiming; a constant attempt to break away that returns with a soft clang each time to the rhyme sound that feels like 'home'. The regular caesuras dotted throughout the poem interrupt the flow clumsily, halting and obstructing the progress both of the speaker's mental working of how to deal with the separation of his child, and the progress of the child's growth and burgeoning independence.

Though the 'I' and 'you' pronouns root this poem in a direct relationship between father and child, speaker and subject, the poem's ending turns, almost embarrassed, away from the full implications of such a direct approach, opting instead for the generalising maxims of 'selfhood' as an abstract concept, 'a walking away' as a generic trope, and 'love' needing to be 'proved' like a clichéd romance tale. Day-Lewis's poem purports to show a 'walking away', a 'letting go', but only really manages to confront the challenges of separation by ignoring them; instead burying itself at its close in truisms, shrugging off the direct confrontation of the changing relationship of father and child, of 'the leaves just turning, / the touch-lines new-ruled'.

Walking Away crunched:

ALMOST – TURNING – SINCE – SATELITTE – AWAY – SCATTER – AWAY – PATHOS – WINDERNESS – PATH – HESITANT – LOOSENED – GRASP – SCORCHING – FIRE – PARTINGS – GNAWS – GOD –SELFHOOD - GO

Charles Causley, *Eden Rock*

Them

The third person plural pronoun is an immediate challenge. It offers a division; a gulf between a 'them' and an 'us'. It suggests distance; there is a physical separation between the speaker, whomever they may be, and the subject of the poem. And it implies a feeling of being left out. A 'they' is a group of people, of which you are by definition not a part. Whether 'they' are in a different place, part of a different group, or partaking in a separate experience, a 'they' is never something that you can become part of; that would by definition transform it into a 'we'.

So, to open the poem with: 'They are waiting for me somewhere beyond Eden Rock' raises a multitude of questions. Though a clear 'me' is established, with a first-person narrative structure set up, it's not immediately clear whether this is a true present, which might seem obvious on looking at the tense of the verb 'they are waiting', or a remembered present, replaying over and over again the old tunes of the past.

'Eden Rock' itself is a deliberately vague location. Charles Causley said he had no idea where it was, as he'd made it up, though he admitted he had told an avid reader that the fictional location was 'probably somewhere in Dartmoor', the national park in Devon. In any case, either the speaker or his parents are 'somewhere beyond' and it is this symbolic locational vagueness rather than the specific location that is important. Important too, of course, is the mythology evoked by the word 'Eden' with its connotations of a perfect world of innocence. In a poem that is almost totally, almost obsessively regular in its form, in terms of the number of stresses in each line and the total number of all syllables, it's surprising how much the first line sticks out. While the vast majority of lines in the poem have ten syllables, giving a rough pentameter, the first line has 13 syllables, giving roughly six stressed syllables. The colon at the end of the line, as opposed to a full stop, also lengthens it, opening the sentence out to the next line and, in a sense, turning its introductory line into the parentheses encapsulating the entire poem.

Father

Causley's description of his father is precise, focussing on the detail of 'the same suit / Of Genuine Irish Tweed', with the age of 'twenty-five' given. With such detail, it's unclear if this is an implication this is a memory – as Causley would likely have been too young to remember much if his father was at this age. Capitalisation of 'Genuine Irish Tweed' carries with it either an implied respect for the brand and its cultural baggage, or sarcasm; a gentle mocking of the perhaps too-intense pride with which his father wore it. The phrase 'same suit' – like 'same three plates' – implies uniformity, but also memory. The suggestion is that these are 'the same plates' and 'the same suit' as on previous occasions. The more specific reference to the 'terrier Jack' who is 'still two years old' seems, however, to diverge from this impression.

The 'still' here sounds like a permanent state; a kind of limbo memory in which the dog is permanently two years old, and the speaker's father is forever wearing the same suit and eating food off the 'same three plates'. The image of the terrier 'trembling at his feet' adds a complicated dimension to the speaker's father. The idea of 'waiting for me' makes the parents seem benevolent, but leaving the dog 'trembling', when taken with the particular

'Genuine Irish Tweed' (capitalised) of the suit, the 'same' suit, creates a more foreboding picture of the man who is perhaps gruff, stern, in control.

Mother

Causley's mother is described in more detail, and with language that has a heightened, metaphorical register. Attractively, her hair is 'the colour of wheat' and 'takes on the light', while her dress is 'sprigged', meaning decorated with patterns of sprigs of leaves or flowers. The image is also more physical. Whereas the description of his father offers only the suit as a fixed physical point of reference, the mother is described by 'the waist', where the dress is 'drawn' in, and 'her hair', sitting underneath the 'straw hat' with a ribbon in it. She is also the first of the pair to take any action, rather than merely being described as if immovable and disconnected to any real-world objects. She 'has spread the stiff white cloth' – whose three stressed syllables make the white cloth feel particularly stiff – 'over the grass' for a picnic.

The everyday details of the third stanza lend the scene a personal touch – specific domestic traditions and family ways of doing things come through to build a unique picture of how the speaker's parents go about their picnic. The tea comes from 'a Thermos', the milk 'straight / From an old H.P. Sauce bottle', with 'a screw / Of paper for a cork'. The care taken is apparent too, as she 'slowly' puts the plates out, and the 'tin cups' have clearly been painted blue at some point – the overall picture is of a very dedicated, but sparse picnic set, a largely DIY, utility affair with the best that can be strung together.

Crossings

The fourth stanza represents a shift in focus. It is the first stanza to open not on people – 'they', 'My mother', 'She', but with 'The sky whitens as if lit by three suns'. This is clearly metaphorical and not literal language. But its potential significance is enormous for deducing the overarching meaning of the poem. The 'three suns' could very easily be the three characters in this carefully arranged and silent tableau – mother, father, and only child – brightening the day with their family picnic. But in a poem that has already dropped hints in a Biblical direction with its title and opening line mentioning 'Eden Rock', it would be hard to ignore any suggestion that the Holy Trinity could be making an appearance.

The 'drifted stream' across which his mother looks could also hold greater significance. Rivers and streams play an important role in literature and mythology because they are two things at once – a barrier to be crossed or surmounted, and a flowing line in themselves – a way to get somewhere, navigate up or downriver, and a passage. So while there is no  clear evidence in the text to suggest such an allusion is being made, it's worth thinking about the stream as more than just a stream. The River Styx in Greek Mythology separated earth from the underworld, where all the dead in ancient Greece supposedly lived. Could it be that Causley is in fact depicting

94

the process of, and difficulty of approaching death?

The father in the poem clearly appears to live life with the relaxation that only the ultimate post-retirement retirement could offer. 'My father spins / A stone along the water', seemingly unbothered about seeking out his son, as the mother does when she 'shades her eyes and looks my way'. The most important word, however, is 'Leisurely'. The line only really has four stressed syllables, rather than the five syllables that are common through the rest of the poem. It hangs off not only the end of the line, its comma trailing off into empty nothingness, but also the end of the stanza. By the time the start of the fifth and final stanza (bar the final extra line break) an aeon may have mentally passed by since the word 'Leisurely,' was actually uttered in reading the poem.

'Beckon' and 'bank' frame the first line of the final stanza, furthering the distance implied between the speaker and his parents with the mention of 'the other bank' of the stream — the stream he must cross if he wants to be reunited with his parents. For them, 'crossing' is the way to be reunited, but he's more cautious. He hears them beckon from the other side, but still waits for them to call out to him, with advice about the flow of the stream.

The final line is the most pivotal of the poem. 'I had not thought that it would be like this,' in the pluperfect tense, throws a spanner into the works of the poem thus far. What is the 'it' the poet's referring to? Is it that the experience of seeing his parents again after a long absence would not be like this? Or dying and entering heaven would not be like this? And, just as importantly, is this statement a positive or negative one? Is the poet saying the 'I had not thought that it would be like this' because it's better than he expected, or because it's failing to meet up to expectations? And why use such an imprecise, unspecific word?

The extra line break – or beginning of a new stanza, depending on your interpretation – further emphasises the distance between Causley and his parents, and his intense awareness of that distance. The half-rhymes, led by the vowels at the end of each line, add to the sense of separation. 'Rock' and 'Jack' don't quite rhyme in the first stanza, but they almost do through their consonance. If the vowels would change, they'd be very close. The rhyming pattern of half-rhythms continues throughout the poem. 'Suit' and 'feet', 'chess' and 'grass', 'hat' and 'light', 'straight' and 'out', 'screw' and 'blue', 'suns' and 'spins', 'way' and 'leisurely', 'bank' and 'think', and finally 'is' and 'this'.

At the start of the poem the parents are 'waiting' for the speaker and at the end of the poem they are left still waiting. The distance that the poem evokes throughout, in its language and in its formal tools, such as the haunting, not-quite there half-rhymes in the text create an intense and almost bleak picture of the distance between him and his parents. So by the time we read that solitary, separate line 'I had not thought that it would be like this,' it already feels like a cry of disappointment.

Eden Rock crunched:

SOMEWHERE – FATHER – GENUINE – STILL – MOHTER – RIBBON – STIFF – LIGHT – POURS – SCREW – SLOWLY – SAME – RUNS – MY – FATHER – LEISURELY – BECKON – HEAR – CROSSING - IT

Seamus Heaney, *Follower*

Probably Seamus Heaney's most famous poem, *Digging*, ends with an image of the poet holding a pen, rather than a spade, in his hand and saying that he intends to 'dig' with it:

'Between my finger and my thumb
The squat pen rests.
I'll dig with it.'

Like *Follower*, *Digging* is a poem about the poet's relationship with his father and about the poet's own sense of identity. Most of *Digging* expresses great admiration for his father's, and his grandfather's, physical strength and dexterity with a spade. However, the last stanza emphasises how the poet is not going to follow his father into the family business of working on a farm. Instead Heaney intends to try to eke out a very different kind of career as a poet. The pen/spade substitution is a characteristic image for Heaney, capturing the central tensions in his relationship to his family, and to his father in particular. It is an image that pulls in two different directions at the same time: On the one hand, it's an image of separation, difference and alteration; Heaney is not following in his father's and grandfather's footsteps. But it is also an image of connection, similarity and continuity; the poet imagines writing to be a form of digging, digging down into the past, into memory, into the mind, in order to find the richest material.

Both *Digging* and *Follower* come from Heaney's first collection of poems *Death of a Naturalist*, published in the late 1960's when the poet was still a young man. Like many writers, Heaney's first published work was broadly autobiographical. The first-person pronoun and the past tense suggest that the narrator of *Follower* is Heaney himself, writing in retrospective voice about a real experience drawn from his childhood. Through memory, the narrator adopts his own childhood perspective, seeing the world through a child's innocent eyes to express undiluted admiration for his father. But in the final two lines there is a distinct change of perspective and of tone, as the narrator's critical, experienced adult voice comes more clearly to the fore and has the final say. As with *Digging*, the poem ends with a twist that suggests the strains in the relationship between farming father and poet son.

Father

Fundamentally, Heaney's father is presented in a favourable light through a small boy's hero-worshiping eyes. In particular, the father's powerful physical presence and his skill in performing a difficult task are emphasised. His size and power is evident from the image of his 'shoulder globed like a full sail strung' where the verb 'globed' subtly alludes to the myth of the Titan, Atlas, holding up the globe. The sense of impressive size and great strength is re-enforced through the simile of the sail, which is 'full'. The overall effect is of a powerful man taking the strain, muscles working hard, up to the task. The later description of the father's 'broad shadow' adds to this impression.

Alongside his physicality, the father's technical adeptness is foregrounded. For example, he controls the horses seemingly effortlessly, with just his 'clicking tongue' and later with just a 'single pluck' of the reins. Thus his easy mastery of powerful natural forces is conveyed. He is also directly and plainly acknowledged as 'an expert' at what he does. Like a doctor or mechanic, the father 'fits' and 'sets' the various parts of the plough. He 'narrowed/ and angled' his eye, 'mapping the furrows', suggesting the task requires concentration: The father is reading the land intelligently and, as the adverb 'exactly' indicates with, reading it with canny precision. His expertise is also signalled through the neat completion of the work; 'the sod rolled over without breaking'. However, beneath this admiration there's a sense of emotional distance between father and son. For example, compared to both a 'sail' and a boat creating a 'wake', the father is dehumanised. And little sense of the father's personality emerges from Heaney's description.

The son

A stark contrast separates the presentation of the father and that of the son. Indeed, they are almost opposites. The father is a master of this labour, he is in tune with and at home in this agricultural context. Heaney is neither:

99

Through repetition, emphasis is placed on his childhood self's physical clumsiness: 'I stumbled'; 'fell sometimes'; 'tripping'; 'falling'. The son also cannot keep up. He is not up to the task, lagging behind his father's 'wake'. Worse, he seems to get in the way of the efficient completion of the work. His presence is an irritant to his father, 'I was a nuisance'. The repetition of three consecutive present continuous verbs 'tripping, falling, yapping' convey annoyance and impatience, with the final one, 'yapping' connoting a small yappy dog. Crucially however, unlike in Digging and despite his apparent ill-suitedness to the task, the son was keen to emulate his father and follow in his footsteps, 'I wanted to grow up and plough'.

Father and son

We've already noted the contrast in the presentation of the principal characters in a poem that can easily be imagined as a short piece of drama. Doing so helps us to notice the quietness, the lack of dialogue, in the scene. The father appears almost silent, utterly absorbed in his task; the only noise he makes is directed at the horses. No dialogue and, though both characters are in the scene, only one point at which they touch. Even then, as the father 'rode' young Heaney on 'his back' to his 'plod' he seems more like a beast of burden, a horse or donkey, than a human.

The 'yapping' and the reference to the son as a 'nuisance' suggests the father's perception, perhaps picked up on by the child, and, as we've noted, implies annoyance. What is the tone of the reversal at the end of the poem? Does the son sound annoyed now that his father 'will not go away'? Or is the tone resigned or frustrated? We cannot tell. But we can say that wanting to be rid of his father sounds harsh, as harsh as the labelling of the over-keen son as a 'nuisance'. Heaney could have picked any memory to present his relationship with his father. He chose this one and ended the poem not with an image of tenderness, mutual understanding or togetherness, but with this unresolved harshness.

The title 'Follower' suggests religious faith or political belief. People only follow something or someone they strongly believe in, apart perhaps on social media. Hence the title contributes to the impression that when he was young, **the son,** like most sons, looked up to his father, desperately wanted to be like him, to continue along the same path. Fathers provide role models of masculinity for their sons and hence are crucial to the forming of their son's identity. For most of the poem this defines himself in relation to his father; he is his follower. However, at some point, sons stop idolising their fathers and begin to see them in a more realistic light. Though the loss of the innocent perspective can be poignant, it can also lead to disillusionment, tension and bitterness. It is, however, an inevitable process we go through as we grow up and struggle to form our own independent identities.

Headrigs etc.

Death of a Naturalist established Heaney's poetic reputation. Later in his career, the poet would go on to win the Nobel Prize for Literature and was frequently called the greatest Irish poet since W.B. Yeats. Heaney's poetic originality lay in his subject matter and in his diction, both of which were 'lowly': Farming life hadn't been considered a suitable topic for the high art form of poetry until Ted Hughes and Heaney made it so. And, though Heaney was fond of tradition poetic forms, the language he employed in his poems, especially his early ones, was often 'unpoetically' rough, conversational and physical. In another poem, *The Ministry of Fear* Heaney refs to his own writing as 'hob-nailed boots' 'from beyond the mountain' 'walking' 'all over the fine lawns' of poetry. Whereas his father's hob-nailed boots walk across the land; Heaney's hob-nailed words across the poetic line. Heaney's great predecessor, Yeats, would never allow common words into the heightened world of his poems. In stark contrast, *Follower* is jam-packed with semi-technical language, conveying the concrete reality of farming equipment: 'shaft'; 'wing'; 'sock'; 'headrig'; 'reins'; 'team'. Yeats also adopted a highly polished, elevated poetic style. The rest of the language in *Follower* is noticeably restrained, plain and straightforward: There is little imagery and use of figurative imagery is especially spare; there are also no complex words – the longest words are disyllabic and many are common monosyllables; the style is uncluttered - adjectives are used sparingly and, when they are, are ordinary and unshowy – 'bright'; 'broad' etc. This simplicity is also reflected in the construction - sentences are connected with the simplest conjunctions, such as 'and' and 'but'.

In fact, the language has very few words derived from Greek, Latin or Romance languages – overwhelmingly Heaney's words are drawn from Anglo-Saxon. The choice of predominantly Anglo-Saxon words, with their plain, down-to-earth physicality matches the poem's subject matter: It is a linguistic parallel, or equivalent, to the work the father is doing. This equivalence is one or a number of ways in which, under the poem's surface, at a subtextual level, the father and son, so seemingly different, are shown to be deeply connected. In this sense, Heaney is, in fact, still following his father's direction, as he was in *Digging*.

As we've noted, a central tension in many of Heaney's poems, is between continuity and change, between honouring the dignity of manual farming labour and a desire to follow a different life path. We see his tension clearly in *Follower*. Notice, for instance, how the movement of the plough is 'back into the land'. Heaney's poetry both follows and deviates from this is inward turning movement. His subject matter - the excavation of his own past, his memories of home, his family and the landscape is an inward movement. But his decision to explore these experiences in poetry is a clear deviation from his almost silent father's footsteps.

We've already noticed that this is a very quiet poem – what imagery there is is mainly visual. This makes the pieces of aural imagery stand out, such as the reference to the father's 'clicking tongue'. Is the controlling of the horses paralleled by the poet's voice controlling the poem's words, and the feelings behind these, perhaps?

Hob-nailedness

With its Anglo-Saxon diction and farming subject, the soundscape of the poem is unsurprisingly heavy, earthy, claggy even. The grounded vocabulary of mono or disyllables - words such as 'sod', 'sock', 'plod', 'stumbled', 'headrig' and 'shoulders' - generates lines that are thick and chunkily textured. This effect is enhanced by the irregularity of both the metre and the rhyme scheme. Though the poem is in common metre - iambic tetrameter - the many deviations from the pattern create an aural and rhymical roughness. This irregular roughness in the poem's flow is signalled from the poem's first line with its double stress ending:

'My father worked with a horse-plough'.

Rhyme too plays its part. Isolate the end rhymes and you'll notice that few of them harmonise and fit together exactly. Most are, in fact, half-rhymes of one form or another, at least in an English accent – we should always bear in mind that Heaney was an Irish poet. A few examples of this sonic roughness should illustrate the point:

'plough' – 'furrow'; 'wing' – 'breaking'; 'sock' – 'pluck'
'eye' – 'exactly'; 'wake' – 'back'; 'plough' – 'follow'

In addition to the end rhymes, the poem is knitted together through vowel sounds (assonance). Variations of 'o' sound predominate. For example, the short 'o' sound runs through 'sod', 'some', 'hob', 'plod', 'sock', and a longer 'o' sound through 'close', 'rode', 'rolled', 'globed', 'furrow', 'narrow'. The 'o' sound finishes in the final rhyme of 'today' and 'away', one of the few full rhymes and hence sonically creates a sense of completion.

My way

Look at the poem on the page. It looks pretty neat and orderly. Six stanzas are arranged tidily in solid and conventional quatrains. Is it too fanciful to suggest that this neat patterning of black shapes on the white background is a poetic version of the father's precision ploughing? Taken with what we've already said about the choice of common metre and plain vocabulary, it seems likely that the correspondence was in the poet's mind. Writing as a form of ploughing of memory.

If this suggestion is accepted, it's further evidence of the subtextual connection between father and son, of deep continuities, underlying

similarities and connections beneath the apparent separation, change and difference. Or, at least, the poet's desire to imply that his writing a form of skilled manual labour, like digging. In relation to the overbearing literary father figure lurking in the background of this poem, W.B. Yeats, Heaney's technique and style also shows that he may have been following in the great poet's broad shadow, but he was also determined to move into the light and go about things in his own way.

Follower crunched:

FATHER – SHOULDERS – FURROW – TONGUE – EXPERT – STEEL-POINTED – SOD – PLUCK – TEAM – ONTO – GROUND – EXACTLY – WAKE – FELL – BACK - PLOD – WANTED – STIFFEN – FOLLOW – SHADOW – NUISANCE – BUT - AWAY

Simon Armitage, *Mother, any Distance*

Book of Matches

This poem is unusual in that it does not have a title, instead it forms part of an anthology of poems entitled 'Book of Matches' in 1993. Each poem within the anthology is designed to be read within the time it takes to strike a match and let it burn down to the end, before you have to blow it out to prevent it from burning you. That is an interesting analogy, and one which provides a useful lens through which we can look at the poem. Armitage intended these poems to capture brief and fleeting moments of human experience, but ones which burn brightly into our consciousness before they disappear. We can certainly apply this to the moment captured in *Mother and distance*, and it is perhaps the brevity of the poem which helps to reinforce its poignancy as a child stretches away from its mother to 'fall or fly'. If you speak to any parent they will tell you that their children only stayed young for what felt like an instant, but that instant burned so brightly it will forever feel like it happened a short time ago.

The brevity of the poem, and the others in the anthology, likens them to sonnets, which often did not have titles but numbers, and are referred to by their first lines, such as Shakespeare's Sonnet 18 *Shall I compare these to a summer's day*. Typically sonnets are 14 lines of iambic pentameter, ending with a rhyming couplet. *Mother any distance* loosely follows this structure, but with an additional line, and the use of trochees rather than iambs. Sonnets also capture these brief moments of human experience, though the subject matter more often focuses on romantic love. The rhyming couplets at the end will then often give a sense of completeness to the moment, perhaps looking to the future and the enduring nature of the love described. The 'endless sky...fall or fly' of the final lines of this poem are certainly reminiscent of the sonnet form, but the lines indicate the end of this phase in the relationship, with the young man moving on alone.

The way the poem parallels many sonnet features but deviates or subverts others could tie in with the overall aims of the poems within his 'Book of Matches' anthology. They express emotions central to the universal human experience, but within Armitage's own modern context. He takes elements of the traditional which are relevant to him, but bends and shapes them to convey his own personal experience. Just like the narrator in his poem, he explores new possibilities and experiences and makes them his own. He has solid foundations, but is not 'anchored' by them - he is more like the 'kite', rooted on solid ground, but free to set his own path.

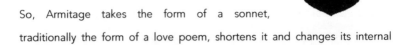

So, Armitage takes the form of a sonnet, traditionally the form of a love poem, shortens it and changes its internal dynamics, such as the conventional metre and rhyme scheme. Technically this shortened or curtailed form of a sonnet is called a 'curtal sonnet'. The idea of the umbilical cord of maternal-child, child-maternal love being cut short or cut off is, of course, the central idea of the poem. Rhymes are, of course, sonic connections within poems. Rhymes cropping up in unexpected places within the poem, sometimes insistently in tight sonic patterns, embody the surprising endurance of the maternal bond. Hence Armitage elegantly and tellingly matches his poem's form to its content.

A second pair of hands

In simple terms, the poem can be described as an extended metaphor, or conceit, whereby the Armitage uses the moment the narrator moves into his own home and needs help with the practicalities of measuring from his mother as a representation of the last time he will really depend on his  mother for that level of support for the rest of his life. Ultimately, the 'second pair of hands' in the future will not belong to his mother, they will belong to his future partner. The fact that these hands could belong to anyone introduces the idea that although he needs his mother now, the role she fills is, in the harshest sense, replaceable. He doesn't need *her* hands he needs *a* pair of hands. This tactile image is evocative of the nurturing and love his mother gave him as a child, and is contrasted later with the 'pinch' of her fingertips, demonstrating how a loving gesture can become oppressive and painful if held for too long.

The formality of the second person address which comes through in the first word 'Mother' conveys the sense perhaps of a difficult conversation lurking behind the poem, one that has needed to happen for a while and one of great importance, that she had to listen to and that the poem subtly re-enacts. He gains her attention and repeats the address with the pronoun 'you' in the third and fifth lines which each begin new sentences describing the support she gives him. There is a sense of sterility in the list of domestic items: 'windows, pelmets, doors', which links to the precise scientific vocabulary used throughout, the 'zero-end' of the tape, 'meters', 'centimeters', 'recording' and 'reporting'. This could reflect the sense that he is trying to keep emotions in check whilst he conveys this message, which is a difficult one for him to say. And for his mother to hear.

Whilst emotions may be tightly controlled, that is not to say they do not exist within the poem. An almost umbilical bond ties the son to his mother, and the two words which sit at the heart of the poem capture the poet's ambivalence about this bond: 'Anchor. Kite.' An anchor offers a place of safety, a fixed point, something that will hold you in place during stormy weather. A kite is anchored to ensure it does not fly too far away, and the person holding that anchor has control over its direction and movement. The freedom of a kite is an illusion; it may have the wind under its wings but it can only fly so far before it is pulled back to earth. An evocative metaphor for the relationship between a parent and a child - they are given increasing amounts of freedom but must always return to 'base'. However, if we take the anchor to refer to the mother and the kite to refer to Armitage we could argue that this is a mixed metaphor; kites don't have anchors, ships have anchors. An anchor for a kite would be like a sledgehammer for a nut. In this subtle way, the two images don't belong as closely together as we might first have thought.

The irregular but somehow-still-rhythmic rhyme scheme is also evocative of the instant closeness of the mother-son relationship at times, and the expansive distance at others. The partial rhyme of "span" and "hands" in the first two lines perhaps reflects the disconnect at the start, mirrored by the formality of the opening address: "Mother". This is followed by the more comfortable 'doors' and 'floors', perhaps as they work well together and enjoy each other's company. The subsequent triple rhyme of the present participles 'recording', 'leaving' and 'unreeling' do not feel so comfortable; there is a sense of constant movement which is repeated too often as the speaker moves further and further away until the rhyme stops abruptly, reinforced by the double end stop of 'Anchor. Kite.' We are then left with just the semblance of a partial rhyme, with the repeated 'i' in 'climb', 'something' and 'give', but it is barely there as the space between the mother and son gapes between them. The 'pinch' of line 12 connects with and almost grasps at the 'reach' of line 13, the final attempt of the mother to keep her son close by. The final, and arguably most poetically beautiful rhyme comes at the end when he gains his freedom: 'sky' links suggestively with 'fly', causing the reader to infer that the narrator is likely to succeed in his adventure.

The mother-son bond is further illustrated through the symbolic use of the tape measure which the mother holds on to while her son unreels the lengths. This metaphor extends across this lengthy sentence which  spans four lines, as the 'years between' them are 'unreeled'. The years have distanced the son from his mother, and whilst this moment between them brings them closer for an instant, now is the time where 'something has to give'. This hints at the strain their relationship has been under, and either the mother needs to let go willingly, or the bond will snap. Her 'fingertips still pinch...the last one hundredth of an inch', demonstrating both her reluctance to let him go and the pain it is ultimately causing him. The final image feels like a tableau with both poised at either end of the house: she two floors below him as he stretches out towards the loft hatch which 'opens on an endless sky'.

Space-walker

There is a strong sense of adventure throughout the poem, with repeated images of what feels like exploration of uncharted territory. The double metaphors in 'acres of the walls, the prairies of the floors' capture the sense of a narrator ready to head out on his own to pastures new; something he finds exciting and terrifying at the same time. His mother's presence is needed initially, possibly to offer reassurance while he finds his

bearings, but as the poem progresses he feels more confident to explore on his own. There is a playfulness around the use of the phrase 'recording...back to base', as if he is a child again and he is a make-believe astronaut with important information the relay. He goes on to 'space-walk' through the 'empty bedrooms' and then 'climb the ladder to the loft' where he reaches towards a 'hatch' which opens on an 'endless sky'. Perhaps this is a game they used to play when he was a child, and they both find comfort in playing it for one last time. There is an unspoken tenderness in the game, and you can almost imagine him jokingly using these childish references to his mother to comfort her as he explains the important message she must hear: this is the last time he will truly be her child, and now he must explore new territory without her supportive but restricting tether.

This sense of exploration is also mirrored in Armitage's use of form, as outlined in the introduction. He takes the security of the traditional sonnet, perhaps his 'anchor', but escapes from the strict confines of it by breaking away from the traditional line length and rhythm. In this sense this poem, and others in his book of matches, reflect the freedom of the 'kite', experimentally taking his poetry in new directions.

Mother any Distance crunched:

MOTHER - ZERO-END - BASE - UNREELING - KITE - SPACE-WALK - BREAKING - GIVE - PINCH - REACH - SKY - FLY

Carol Ann Duffy, *Before You Were Mine*

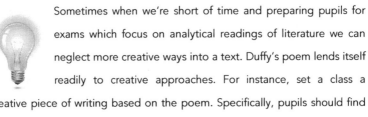 Sometimes when we're short of time and preparing pupils for exams which focus on analytical readings of literature we can neglect more creative ways into a text. Duffy's poem lends itself readily to creative approaches. For instance, set a class a creative piece of writing based on the poem. Specifically, pupils should find some old photographs of relatives of theirs [it doesn't have to be their mother and probably will work better with a grandparent or great aunt or uncle] picking three or four as their main focus. They should then think of a memory they associate with this person and a couple of objects with special significance, what Duffy calls 'relics'. Their task then is to write at least a couple of paragraphs describing this person and their feelings about them, both positive and negative. As this is potentially a revealing, personal experience, I'd recommend you only mark the work if pupils would like you to.

The piece justifies itself as descriptive and reflective writing, but it can also be used to illuminate Duffy's poem and to help pupils write about an aspect of poetry they often find challenging – the impact of form and structure. For instance, though it's arranged on the page in neatish looking stanzas, *Before You Were Mine* doesn't have either a regular metre or a rhyme scheme. Whisper it about a poem by the poet laureate if you dare, but is this poem really prose just chopped up and arranged neatly to look like a poem? What might save it from such an accusation? Well, the poem would have to have clear benefits from the way it has been arranged on the page. In other words, the lineation and stanza form must actively contribute to its effects, otherwise it really is just prose disguised to look like poetry. A great, active way for pupils to investigate the significance of form is to present it first to them as prose and to set them the task of arranging it into whatever lines and stanzas they think would work best. To break the task down a little, they could read the first couple of stanzas, re-arranged as prose, as shown below. Their task is then try to package the words back into a first stanza. Once they've had a go, swap examples, show them Duffy's choice and then challenge them to predict the shape of the subsequent stanzas.

Before You Were Mine's first two stanzas prosefied:

I'm ten years away from the corner you laugh on with your pals, Maggie McGeeney and Jean Duff. The three of you bend from the waist, holding each other, or your knees, and shriek at the pavement. Your polka-dot dress blows round your legs. Marilyn. I'm not here yet. The thought of me doesn't occur in the ballroom with the thousand eyes, the fizzy, movie tomorrows the right walk home could bring. I knew you would dance like that. Before you were mine, your Ma stands at the close with a hiding for the late one. You reckon it's worth it.

This task foregrounds the issue of regularity. What might be gained, for instance, by varying the number of lines in the second stanza? And what is, in fact, gained by Duffy's arrangement? Which words gain a little bit of extra stress by the way they are placed on the page? Where does Duffy uses enjambment to link across lines and where does she use caesura to break lines and sentences up. Now when you show the class the whole poem they are more likely to be keyed into aspects of form, more likely to notice the consistency of the stanza pattern and already be engaged in thinking about its effect and significance.

If they're not used to this sort of task, your students might find it helpful be given some examples of how the sentences could be possibly be arranged in poetic form:

Arrangement #1; Duffy dons her Emily Dickinson disguise:

I'm ten years away from the corner
you laugh on with your pals -

Maggie McGeeney and Jean Duff -
The three of you bend from the waist

holding each other, or your knees -
and shriek at the pavement.

Your polka-dot dress blows round -
your legs - Marilyn. I'm not here yet.

The thought of me doesn't occur -
in the ballroom with the thousand eyes.

Arrangement #2; Duffy does concrete poetry:

I'm
ten years
away from the corner you laugh
on with your pals, Maggie McGeeney
and Jean Duff. The three of

you bend

from the waist
,holding each

other,   or your knees,
and   shriek   at the pavement.
Your polka-dot dress   blows   round

your legs.
Marilyn.
I'm not here
yet.

With these possibilities in mind, let's consider Duffy choices of lineation. The most obvious benefit the poet gains from her arrangement of the poem into five line stanzas [cinquains] is a sense of order and control. Each of the images, all the memories, the poet's or persona's* feelings, those of her mother, her friends, her clothes and so forth are all boxed and contained within robust-looking stanza frames. The fact that each of these frames is five lines long is a signal that unbroken, unchanging order has been imposed on the unruly, hazy stuff of memory. This impression is enhanced by the fact that each stanza is also complete unto itself; each one ending with either an emphatic full stop or a question mark.

Duffy's lineation also makes the full stops more obvious and pronounced. There are four of them in just the first stanza all appearing at the end of lines. In the first case, after 'on' they allow the reader a moment to reflect on the potential significance of the opening two lines. The double full stops in the last line, after both 'legs' and 'Marilyn' help create a sense of separate snapshots of the mother the poet is stringing together into a narrative. That last word is also, of course, an incomplete or truncated sentence. So, if the stanza form of the poem signals order, here we have the opposite, the rules of syntax breaking down. Finally, the lineation also allows Duffy to give important words a bit more of a push than they would have in a prose version. The most significant example is that final word, 'Marilyn', stuck on its own, isolated at the end of the stanza.

As we have noted, the stanza form gives the impression of neat, controlled order imposed on the material and, in particular, on its subject, the mother, while other elements run counter to this pattern. As well as the syntax, there is a lack of a regular metre. There is no set number of beats per line and the lines also have different numbers of syllables, ranging in the whole poem from the shortest [10] to the longest [17]. There is something about this material, it seems, that resists the attempt to box and trim it into shape. Tonally, too, the poem is uncertain, difficult to pin down. The opening images of the mother and her friends depict them in an uncomplicated way, having fun together. But these images are preceded and

117

shadowed by the poet's presence 'I'm ten years away'. And isn't there something a little creepy and unnerving about the poet's unseen presence, silently watching her oblivious mother's carefree behaviour? Something rather voyeuristic? Something a little like a security camera? And though the comparison of the mother with the glamorous actress Marilyn Monroe might at first appear to be flattering, Monroe was a famously troubled sex symbol who

committed suicide. The poet doesn't divulge clues as to her feelings so we don't know how to take that stark label 'Marilyn'. Could the tone, in fact, be accusatory or envious?

Sweetheart

Certainly, the mother is presented in other ways that also connote glamour as well as energy and self-confidence. Her clothes, for instance, such as the 'polka-dot dress' and her 'high-heeled red shoes'. She is a 'bold girl', 'winking', attending dances at ballrooms, having fun with her mates, unabashed. Her life seems full of promise of a bright future, 'fizzy movie tomorrows'. The adjective here suggests fun, childhood and ebullience and is echoed in 'sparkle', while the reference to 'movies' accords with the image of Monroe. The fact that the ballroom has a 'thousand eyes' and the mother has 'small bites on her neck' imply popularity and romance. As does the word 'sweetheart'. But this affectionate noun is not employed in the poem by a potential lover, but transgressively and unnervingly by the poet narrator. This implies she has feelings towards the mother more usually associated with those of a lover. In this light, other images, such as the 'lovebites' suggest an edgy jealousy, particularly as this image is couched as a question 'whose small bites?'

Mine

We mentioned earlier that Duffy's poem could be read either broadly autobiographically, expressing the poet's feelings about her mother, or if we take the narrator to be a persona, it could be read as a dramatic monologue. Either way, the narrator of the poem, seeing but unseen, is a rather unsettling, ominous, even threatening presence. There's something egocentric, for example, about the way they top and tail the poem with themselves ['I'm'; 'mine'], as if everything, including their mother's life before they were born, now starts and ends with them. Then there's the repeated, possessive phrase 'before you were mine', and its echo in 'I wanted'. Add to that the unnerving phrases we have already noted and others, such as calling

the mother a 'ghost' as if she is dead already, or 'I see you, clear as scent', which could either innocently suggest perfume or more disturbingly the scent of an animal being tracked and hunted. Think of how the latter might tie in with the overall sense of invisible surveillance. Then there's the implication of the poem's final sentence, 'that glamorous love lasts / where you sparkle and waltz and

laugh before you were mine'; surely all the fun and freedom is over now. Consider too the very firm imposition of control and order and we arrive, perhaps, at something close to the sort of pathological jealousy we saw in Browning's *Porphyria's Lover*. Or are we being too melodramatic? Is Duffy just being honest about how having a child can affect a parent's, and specifically a mother's, life and about how possessively a child's love for their mother can be? We'll leave that up to you to decide.

Before you were Mine crunched:

I'M – PALS – THREE – SHRIEK – MARILYN – YET – TOMORROWS – I – BEFORE – WORTH – YELL – RELICS – GHOST – SCENT – BITES – HOME – WRONG – WANTED – LASTS - MINE

Owen Sheers, *Winter Swans*

Skirrid

Taken from an anthology of his poems entitled 'Skirrid Hill', *Winter Swans* is one of the few poems in the collection which offer a sense of togetherness and unification. 'Skirrid' comes from the Welsh 'Ysgariad', which literally means divorce or separation, and most the poems in his anthology represent what critic Sarah Crown refers to as a 'fractured emotional landscape'[3]. Relationships disintegrate, people move apart, in a manner not unlike Armitage describes in *Mother Any Distance*. This poem offers a contrast to the overriding theme of his poetry, and in this sense, it is somehow special and different to the rest. Whilst the couple described have spent time 'silent and apart', they are able to find a way to move on together. They are unique in the context of the other relationships in his anthology, perhaps a representation of the manner in which so many relationships come to an end. Think about all the relationships you have experienced in your lives: friendships, groups you've belonged to, family

---

[3] https://www.theguardian.com/books/2006/feb/25/featuresreviews.guardianreview28

members you have lost. Over time there are very few relationships which withstand the test of time, either because we move on as people, those we love pass on, or we experience conflict that is left unresolved. Whilst this can be sad and difficult to think about, ultimately it means that those relationships we do keep hold of are very special, particularly if we are able to resolve our differences and move onwards together.

The waterlogged earth

Sheers has established himself as a poet of Wales, a country of outstanding natural beauty. Akin to Heaney and his strong roots in Ireland, and Wordsworth and his passion for the Lake District, Sheers uses the natural landscape he grew up in as inspiration for much of his writing. The strong connection between man and nature is clear in *Winter Swans*, with the weather and its impact on the natural landscape acting as a metaphor for the couple's relationship. The opening 'clouds' that 'had given their all' appear to represent the two people who have fought tirelessly, 'two days of rain' reflecting the conflict between them and the tears that have been shed. Each line ends at the point at which the speaker may take a breath 'breath breaks', which are frequent at the start of the poem but generally

become longer as the poem progresses. This suggest the weariness of the poetic voice at the outset of the poem, they are tired of the time spent quarrelling and the pace is therefore slow and plodding as they take a moment's pause from the ongoing argument.

Conflict between the couple is not, however, the central focus of the poem. There is no discussion or analysis of the cause; this appears now irrelevant and is cast aside within the first line and a half. The abrupt 'and then a break' feels a little disjointed, as if they have said all there is to say, shed all the tears there are to shed, and, although they have not reached a resolution, they have realised the time has come to stop. The sense that they have been drowning in their sorrow is reflected in the 'waterlogged earth' which is 'gulping for breath' at their feet. Representing the sense of disillusionment that has worn them down and caused them to become stuck in their negative emotions, the image is of mud that is difficult to wade through, clogging up their path. However, from this negative image springs a sense of hope: the fact that it is 'gulping for breath' shows that there is a desire there to keep breathing, to keep the relationship alive.

It is the swans in the subsequent stanza which 'tipping in unison' appear to behave in a way which gives the couple a signal, a sign that they can move forward in their relationship. The swans seem to experience difficulties, 'rolling weights down their bodies', dipping into 'dark water' before rising to the surface 'like boats righting in rough weather'. They endure hardships, but they face them together, as one. This is reinforced by the addressee of the poem who comments that 'They mate for life', the implication being that the couple are married and have promised to do the same. The observation is immediately followed by a description of the 'stilling water', continuing the metaphor set up at the start. But this time there is calm after the storm. 'Afternoon light' offers a sign of future promise as they 'moved on through' it. At this point the lines expand in length; if initially the speaker was weary and plodding, and the lines, like stilted conversation, hard to sustain, now they are charged with renewed energy and life and the ability to articulate thought.

The two metaphorical images of the weather and the swans combine in the final couplet where their hands 'swum the distance between us' and 'folded...like a pair of wings settling after flight'. The 'waterlogged earth' at the start of the poem no longer creates a barrier between them; rather the water provides the path through which they can find each other again. Their hands become a harmonious pair of wings, an homage to the swans who acted as the catalyst for their reunion.

Icebergs of white feather

The use of colour throughout the poem helps to reinforce the sense of distance and then coming together. The clouds that had 'given their all' initially create a grey and dismal landscape, reinforced by the 'two days of rain'. In the following stanza the 'gulping' earth muddies this dismal landscape, with its washed-out palette of grey and brown. The bleak descriptions of the setting mirror the emotions of the couple; their relationship lacks colour, the 'two days of rain' have drained this away, leaving them gloomy and despondent.

The swans suggest an opportunity for the couple to see this break in their conflict as a fresh chance to start again: their 'icebergs of white feather' are pure and clean, a blank slate upon which they can renew their relationship. There is a strong juxtaposition between the 'dark water' and the 'white' of the swans. Whilst black and white mixed together create grey, the swans do not become grey in the blackened (perhaps muddied) waters. This could offer a symbol for the couple; the swans do not allow the dirt and grime of the life they lead to soil them, they emerge from the dark water fresh and clear. Perhaps the conflict the couple have experienced relates to external pressures: most couples can identify with the way in which life can get in the way of their relationship, and how arguments can arise from people and events on the 'outside'. The metaphorical reference to 'porcelain' to describe the silent elegance of the swans as they swim away reinforces the way in which they rise above the turbulence which surrounds them; porcelain is a pure white ceramic, often used to create objects of great beauty and value. This image emphasises how the purity of the swan's companionship is to be revered. It is an image reminiscent of the sublime: a greatness beyond all possibility of calculation, measurement or imitation.

Only once the couple have observed the swans does the landscape fill with 'afternoon light'. Now they are able to appreciate the 'shingle and sand'

which is illuminated. Shingle and sand are often made up of a multitude of colours, and sand particularly conjures up images of golden horizons. The couple have left behind the 'waterlogged earth' and can now 'slow-step' onto the surer ground. There's a tentativeness about this description, however, as shingle and sand are not solid. They need to 'slow-step', but they are doing it together, not 'silent and apart' as at the start of the poem. The final metaphorical reference to their hands which become like a 'pair of wings', as well as completing the homage to the swans, also completes the colour palette of the poem. The wings are white, and their joined hands represent the fresh beginning the couple are embarking upon, together.

Winter Swans crunched:

CLOUDS - RAIN - WALKED - EARTH - GULPING - APART - SWANS - UNISON - WEIGHTS - DARK - ICEBERGS - RIGHTING - MATE - PORCELAIN - LIGHT - SLOW-STEPPING - HANDS - DISTANCE - FOLDED - WINGS

Daljit Nagra, *Singh Song!*

Standard English

noun

The form of the English language widely accepted as the usual correct form: "children often use native forms at home and speak standard English at school".

As Eric Falci writes in *The Cambridge Introduction to British Poetry, 1945-2010*, Daljit Nagra writes 'linguistically exuberant poems about the experience of Indian immigrants in Britain'.[4] Specifically, Nagra's rejects the constraints of Standard English [SE], writing instead in what Falci calls a 'Punjabi-inflected English vernacular' and others have termed 'Punglish', a phonetic (spelt-as-it-sounds) hybrid language suggesting Punjabi pronounciation of English. Glance over this poem, the concluding one in Nagra's breakthrough collection 'Look We Have Coming to Dover!', and you'll spot many words that are spelt as they sound in Indian English rather than spelt 'correctly' following SE. Here is a sprinkling: 'ov', 'di', 'vunt', 'hav',

---

[4] The Cambridge Introduction, p.211

'vee', 'luv', 'vid', 'yoo', 'bin', 'dat' and 'yen'. Other aspects of Punglish include the omission of articles, such as 'the' or 'a' as well as non-standard verb forms.

The obvious, central relationships in Nagra's poem are family based; relationships between the enamoured narrator and his crew-cutted bride, between the narrator and his father and the bride and both parents. To this list we can add the relationship between the narrator and his customers. More subtle, however, is the relationship between the poem and the language and the culture of which it is part. All these relationships share one thing however; they defy expectations and bust stereotypes. And do so with great, exuberant gusto.

Tartan saris

Our unabashed narrator defies the convention of the good, dutiful, hard-working Indian son, carefully looking after the family business, here the traditional corner shop. Newly married, his mind is certainly rarely on this job; he is not taking care of the shop because he's more interested in taking care of ['making luz', 'di tickle ov'] his new bride. Society's disapproval of his errant behaviour is expressed via his complaining customers, who, in a catchy comic refrain, label the shop 'di worst Indian shop/ in di whole Indian road'. Nor does our dreamy-minded narrator show any modesty about his private life; there's a frank relish of his sensual, sexual pleasures in his description, for instance, of intercourse as like 'rowing through Putney'.

His new wife defies racial, social and cultural norms in an even bolder style. She is about as far as she could get from the image of a demure, dutiful and elegant blushing bride. Upstairs she's already flicking through dating sites,

128

putting her own modern spin on the idea of arranged marriages. Rather than honouring and respecting her in-laws she treats them with undisguised disdain, ridiculing and laughing at her father-in-law and shockingly 'effing at' her mother-in-law in 'all di colours of Punjabi'. If her behaviour is unconventional, so too is her appearance. With her eyes like a 'gun' and stomach like a 'teddy', she deviates markedly from accepted notions of beauty. The gun image, of course, suggests that she is potentially dangerous and powerful, while the 'teddy' implies that she may be warm and cuddly, but also somewhat rotund, perhaps. Moreover, her hair cut and  clothes add to the sense of cultural rebellion. Sporting an unfeminine, punky 'red crew cut' the bride wears a masculine 'donkey jacket' over her sari. The incongruity of her language and appearance match her husband's out-of-placeness as a shopkeeper and both aspects add to the poem's humorous effect.

However, like her husband who runs a corner shop rather than, for instance, working as a butcher or professional footballer, the wife does not break entirely from her cultural heritage. The fact she continues to wear a sari, in particular, captures the hybrid nature of her identity. That she is still wearing a sari indicates an identification with Indian culture; the fact that the sari is 'tartan' underlines her affinity with Western, and specifically punk sub-culture. This woman is Indian English, and Indian English in her own stereotype-busting, exuberant and idiosyncratic way.

An Indian music hall song

Nagra's poem is called a song and it certainly has some, sonorous [song-like] qualities. We have, for instance, several voices – the narrator's, his wife's and those of the customers. These voices perform variously as solos, in a duet and as a sort of chorus. Added to this, the poem seems to zip along on short lines with frequent, often comic end-rhymes. The first stanza, for example, has three out of four lines end-rhyming; 'shops'-'clock'-'lock' and the second rhymes 'chapatti' with 'chutney' and 'Putney'. Another pattern of song-like repetition is evident in recurring phrases, such as 'Ven I', 'my bride' and 'from di stool'.

But this is no regular, familiar sort of love song. Though his poem has distinct sections and developments like a piece of music and motifs common to love songs, such as the moon, Nagra deviates from poetic conventions such as metre. His poem sets off regularly enough in a four beat, four-line stanza or quatrain. But by only the second stanza the poem has already broken loose of this conventional pattern: the second stanza has five lines and the middle lines slip free of tetrameter. The next stanza has eight lines and then we're back to a quatrain, but this time with much longer, slower lines. The last eight lines of the poem are arranged as couplets and the  typological trick of indenting some lines is repeated here. Noticeably here the poem slows and takes on a more romantic style as the two lovers perform a little, tender duet while watching that eternal, conventional symbol of love, the moon.

Perhaps the shifting, unstable, but energetic form of the poem also reflects the character of a narrator unable to exert control over his shop, his new wife or his own enthusiastic impulses.

Metrically and in terms of stanza form, the poem's a mish-mash, a car-crash. To the poetry purist this might seem intolerably erratic and technically messy – the linguistic equivalent of mixing oil and water paint, or, if we also factor in the Punglish, roast beef and Yorkshire puds with prawn korma and naan bread. Or, of course, English vocabulary with Indian pronounciation. And, however the snooty purist might object, the point is that it works - the poem has a winning breezy comic momentum and a distinct, original poetic voice.

All the features we've identified contribute to the poem's energy. But equally important are the sentence construction, the punctuation and the use of caesura and enjambment. Sweep the poem to find its first definitive full stop, for instance, and you'll come up empty-handed. In fact, the first sentence runs over twelve lines and the whole poem comprises four sentences, at most. The most common punctuation mark is a loosely linking one, the hyphen and the last line ends with a sense of incompletion, or continuation. This is a long poem, yet there's not a single caesura to break the onward flow of the lines. Instead enjambment of lines and stanzas helps generate a sense of words surfing their own wave, of vibrant energy just about kept in check by narrative momentum.

Like the title, which puts an Indian spin on the idea of good, old fashioned 'sing song' and the new bride's sari, the poem's form and its diction are hybrid. Nagra is writing within and against English poetic convention. As Falci says Nagra 'maps the complexity of a hybrid belonging, when one is caught among identities, languages, cultural practices and racial categories'. Reading *Singh Song!*, however, 'caught' sounds unduly negative. As the exclamation-mark of the title signals from the get to, Nagra's dramatic monologue is surely ebullient and celebratory, the poet surely revelling in the freedom to pick and mix from the rich variety of two or more cultures, riding the wave of energy generated by the cultural collision.

Singh Song! crunched:

DADDY'S – 9 O'CLOCK – BREAK – BUT – BRIDE – SHARE – CHUTNEY – LUV – ROWING – PINNIE – SHOPPERS – VER – LIMES – PLAINTAIN – DISRTY – WORST – INDIAN – HEEL – WEB – LOVER – PRICE – BRIDE – EFFING – COLOURS – DRUNK – FUN – BRIDE – GUN – TEDDY – BRIDE – CREW – TARTAN – DONKEY – PINCHING – TICKLE – CRY – VER – DATE – STALE – STOCK – WORST – WHOLE – MIDNIGHT – QUIET – CONCRETE-COOL – SILVER – BARS – VEE – MOON – EACH – BABY – NIGHT – COST – SAY – BABY – SAY – PRICELESS.

A crunchier crunch:

DADDY'S – BRIDE – LUV – SHOPPERS – DRUNK – TARTAN – MIDNIGHT – MOON – BABY – PRICELESS

Andrew Waterhouse, *Climbing my Grandfather*

Random word generating

From the 1970s onwards the rock star David Bowie used various randomising techniques to produce song lyrics. By the 1990s Bowie had developed a computer programme, The Verbaliser, to help generate unusual combinations of words and phrases and produce unique lyrics. Bowie had picked up this approach from literary writers who wanted to produce original works by breaking the constraining patterns of ordinary language. To develop new perceptions and insights, so the thinking went, a writer had to shatter conventional ways of seeing which are encoded in and re-enforced by the language we use. Clichés are obvious examples of how, over time, language tends to fall into familiar, deadened patterns. The term 'collocation' refers to wider familiar patterns of language. If, for example, I say 'fish and' you will probably think of 'chips'. With their name the band *The Artic Monkeys* break collocation by putting together words that don't conventionally belong together.

One way of understanding [and producing] poems is as collisions of different lexical fields. Waterhouse's poem, for instance, splices together language describing the poet's grandfather with the language of climbing and mountain terrain. There's a couple of ways to produce a poem using this sort of splicing. As Ray Cluey illustrated in The English and Media Centre's emagazine 65 a few years back, a simple way is to pick two subjects that are unrelated, such as eating a peach and a Maths lesson, perhaps. Ideally one topic will encourage sensory description and the other writing that is more abstract. In a classroom setting, it's best to introduce the first topic, but not the second, so that the splicing genuinely throws up surprising results. First pupils have to write 4 or 5 lines on topic A, eating a peach in my example, in which each line is a sentence or a clause. Then they repeat the process with topic B, my Maths lesson. Finally, they splice together words and phrases from both A and B to create their poem. For the second method pupils should choose three separate topics, such as a favourite hobby, gardens and politics. Next they should write up to twenty words and phrases that they associate with each of these topics, i.e. language from that lexical field. Once they have written out their three word lists they could increase the randomising factor by swapping one list with a partner. Now they need to cut out all the words and place them into three piles, one for each topic. Turning the pieces of paper face down, so that they can't see the words, pupils pluck one piece of paper at random from each pile, turn over and write down whatever they've got. They can choose any word order and they can add function words, prefixes and suffixes, pluralise and change tense, but they should keep the main sense of the original words. They should then repeat the produce until all the words have been used up. The final stage is picking out the best ten lines and working these up into a poem. Simples.

Climbing up, into the light

Musician, environmentalist and writer Andrew Waterhouse [1958-2001] won the prestigious Forward Poetry Prize for best first collection with 'IN' in 2000. Great things were expected to follow. Tragically, however, Waterhouse suffered from depression and committed suicide only a year later. His friend

and fellow poet, Linda France, has commented that 'there are a lot of cul-de-sacs and confined spaces in his work'. One way and another, there is also a lot of darkness. Hence, maybe, this is why the poem celebrates the freedom of climbing and specifically climbing in open spaces, upwards to a summit where the exhausted poet watches symbols of freedom, 'birds' and 'clouds' circling in the sky. Waterhouse's sense of joy and exaltation from climbing into the light also reflects his tender feelings about, and admiration for, his grandfather.

Trying to get a grip

In Waterhouse's obituary in The Guardian, fellow poet Sean O'Brien commented that the 'world' of Waterhouse's poetry is 'full of solid objects and hard edges – stones, wood, frozen ground, which offer little purchase to its inhabitants'. Purchase is essential to this poem. Purchase in the sense of being connected to something or someone that gives the poet a hold on his life and on his own troubling emotions. This solid on which he can lean and depend on and orientate himself around is provided by his grandfather. Indeed, that verb, 'purchase', is used in the line about the grandfather's nails 'giving good purchase'. Waterhouse was clearly in desperate need of finding something to hold on to. The psychological dimension of this need is evident from the common use of the phrase 'trying to get a grip'. People try to get a grip when they feel life is sliding away from them, or when they feel a need to exhort themselves to make a stronger effort to control their own feelings. Other phrases within the poem, such as 'pull myself up', 'move on' and 'not looking down' enhance the idea that the climbing metaphor for Waterhouse conveys a mental need to force himself out of difficult and dark emotions. 'Climbing' up his grandfather the poet climbs up out of mental anguish.

If most of the world seemed to the poet to be composed of hard, cold unforgiving surfaces and edges, then the grandfather provided the opposite. Adjectives used about him imply comforting, close contact. The poet is able to 'push into the weave' of his trousers; the skin of the old man's finger is 'smooth and thick' and, crucially, 'warm'; the skin of his next is 'loose'; his wrinkles are 'easy' and his hair is 'thick' and 'soft'. Noticeably, several the details share broken surfaces: The shoes, for instance, are 'cracked', the nails are 'splintered', the arm has a 'ridge', the cheek is compared to 'scree'. Perhaps these surfaces are comforting because they are not smooth, blank walls; instead their unevenness offers exactly the sort of purchase the poet needs.

Obviously, the whole poem comprises an extended metaphor, or conceit, comparing the grandfather to a mountain or cliff face. Turning his relation into such a monumental, giant, timeless figure signals this figure's huge importance in the poet's life. The unbroken, tower-like form of the poem further emphasises this impression. And through contact with this giant figure the poet can lift himself up, lift his spirits up to a summit where he can rest and recuperate.

Climbing has its dangers

If 'climbing' his grandfather is such a positive, enabling experience why then does the poet say it might be dangerous? At the start of the poem he tells us he is going to free climb, i.e. climb without the safety of 'rope' or 'net'. This is a choice the poet makes, so it appears that this danger is essential to the experience in some way. Perhaps getting so close up to his grandfather might activate otherwise dormant feelings of grief, particularly if the poem is prompted by childhood memories of when adults seemed huge and particularly if the grandfather is now dead. Perhaps too there's a sense in which writing about someone you love is also a dangerous act in itself. That person, or other members of your family, might disagree with the poet's portrait of them, might even object to being appropriated to art. Especially so if the grandfather wasn't alive and able to grant his permission. And, maybe, there's the danger of unearthing unflattering details about a relative's life and expressing the writer's true feelings about them. Depression is sometimes described as feeling as 'down', 'low' and 'dark' as it is possible to go. The other danger of climbing, of course, is of falling back downwards into the dark.

So far we've suggested that the poem expresses Waterhouse's love and admiration for his grandfather. But might there be another way of reading it? We could cite in evidence the odd, almost paradoxical way that the grandfather's 'warmth' is compared to 'ice'. We could add that the ridge of the scar also suggests a slippery, cold surface, being described as 'glassy'. We might note that his hand is described as 'stained'. And those surfaces we have suggested are valuable because they provide crucial purchase could be read as rough and bluff, and, well, as just that, as surfaces. The poet's engagement with the grandfather is a struggle and he only ever reaches a rough surface level of intimacy – there is little sense of the grandfather as a person. Finally, we could reconsider the mountain conceit. Yes, mountains are majestic, grand, monumental, unchanging, timeless and so forth. But they are also not human; often they are hard, cold, rocky, potentially dangerous places. In choosing to compare his grandfather to a mountain Waterhouse dehumanises him. This giant figure is entirely oblivious to the poet's presence, its pupils opening and closing and not registering him at all. Furthermore, in relation to his grandfather, the poet presents himself as a tiny, pathetic, infantilised figure. At a push, we could suggest the complete lack of rhyme in the poem is also significant in this way, for rhyme crucially creates sonic links between words and generates sonic harmony. Such a pervasive absence of rhyme surely signals a lack of connection.

Agree? Disagree? Why?

Such a strongly negative reading goes against the grain of the last, concluding lines of the poem. These lines convey a sense of intimacy, both physical 'feeling the heat' and mental 'knowing'. Moreover, there is a close emotional bond and uncomplicated celebration in the reference to a 'good heart'. So, the poem is not entirely sentimental; it doesn't merely present the grandfather and the poet's relationship with him in the warm, fuzzy glow of mutual affection, it's more nuanced and realistic than that. Crucially too, as we have noted, this was a poet who desperately needed things to hold onto in life and the constant, monumental figure of his grandfather certainly provided that security.

Climbing my Grandfather crunched:

FREE – CRACKED – EASY – GRIP – OVERHANGING – TRAVERSE – STAINED – PURCHASE – SMOOTH – WARM – SCAR – GENTLY – FIRM – DOWN – DANGERS – LOOSE – SMILING – SCREED – STARE – UP – WRINKLES – SOFT – SUMMIT – BREATH – BIRDS – FEELING – HEART

A sonnet of revision activities

1. Reverse millionaire: 10,000 points if students can guess the poem just from one word from it. You can vary the difficulty as much as you like. For example, 'clams', would be fairly easily identifiable as from Sexton's poem whereas 'fleet' would be more difficult. 1000 points if students can name the poem from a single phrase or image – 'portion out the stars and dates'. 100 points for a single line. 10 points for recognising the poem from a stanza. Play individually or in teams.

2. Research the poet. Find one sentence about them that you think sheds light on their poem in the anthology. Compare with your classmates. Or find a couple more lines or a stanza by a poet and see if others can recognise the writer from their lines.

3. Write a cento based on one or more of the poems. A cento is a poem constructed from lines from other poems. Difficult, creative, but also fun, perhaps.

4. Read 3 or 4 other poems by one of the poets. Write a pastiche. See if classmates can recognise the poet you're imitating.

5. Write the introduction for a critical guide on the poems aimed at next year's yr. 11 class.

6. Practice comparing and contrasting: Write the name of each poem on a separate card. Turn face down and mix up the cards. Turn back over any three cards at random. What do two of the poems have in

common? How is the third one different? Replace the cards and do the exercise again.

7. Use the poet Glynn Maxwell's typology of poems to arrange the poems into different groups. In his excellent book, *On Poetry*, Maxwell suggests poems have four dominant aspects, which he calls solar, lunar, musical and visual. A solar poem hits home, is immediately striking. A lunar poem, by contrast, is more mysterious and might not give up its meanings so easily. Ideally a lunar poem will haunt your imagination. Written mainly for the ear, a musical poem focuses on the sounds of language, rather than the meanings. Think of Lewis Carroll's *Jabberwocky*. A visual poem is self-conscious about how it looks to the eye. Concrete poems are the ultimate visual poems. According to Maxwell the very best poems are strong in each dimension. Try applying this test to each poem. Which ones come out on top?

8. Maxwell also recommends conceptualising the context in which the words of the poem are created or spoken. Which poems would suit being read around a camp fire? Which would be better declaimed from the top of a tall building? Which might you imagine on a stage? Which ones are more like conversation overheard? Which are the easiest and which the most difficult to place?

9. Mr Maxwell is a fund of interesting ideas. He suggests all poems dramatise a battle between the forces of whiteness and blackness, nothingness and somethingness, sound and silence, life and death. In each poem what is the dynamic between whiteness and blackness? Which appears to have the upper hand?

10. Maxwell argues too that the whiteness is a different thing for different poems. Consider each poem's whiteness in the light of this idea. See any differences?

11. Still thinking in terms of evaluation, consider the winnowing effect of time. Which of these poems do you think might be still read in 20, a 100 or 200 years? Why?

12. Give yourself only the first and last line of one of the poems. Without peeking at the original, try to fill in the middle. Easy level: write in prose. Expert level: attempt verse.

13. According to Russian Formalist critics poetry performs a 'controlled explosion on ordinary language'. What evidence can you find in this selection of controlled linguistic detonations?

14. A famous musician once said that though he wasn't the best at playing all the notes, nobody played the silences better. In Japanese garden water features the sound of a water drop is designed to make us notice the silence around it. Try reading one of the poems in the light of these comments, focusing on the use of white space, caesuras, punctuation – all the devices that create the silence on which the noise of the poem rests.

15. In *Notes on the Art of Poetry*, Dylan Thomas wrote that 'the best craftsmanship always leaves holes and gaps in the works of the poem so that something that is not in the poem can creep, crawl, flash or thunder in'. Examine a poem in the light of this comment, looking for

its holes and gaps. If you discover these, what 'creeps', 'crawls' or 'flashes' in to fill them?

16. Different types of poems conceive the purpose of poetry differently. Broadly speaking Augustan poets of the eighteenth century aimed to impress their readers with the wit of their ideas and the elegance of the expression. In contrast, Romantic poets wished to move their readers' hearts. Characteristically Victorian poets aimed to teach the readers some kind of moral principle or example. Self-involved, avant-garde Modernists weren't overly bothered about finding, never mind pleasing, a general audience. What impact do the AQA anthology poems seek to have? Do they seek to amuse, appeal to the heart, teach us something? Are they like soliloquies – the overheard inner workings of thinking – or more like speeches or mini-plays? Try placing each poem somewhere on the following continuums. Then create a few continuums of your own. As ever, comparison with your classmates will prove illuminating.

Emotional..intellectual

Feelings...ideas

Internal...external

Contemplative...rhetorical

Open..guarded

NB
Yes, we know. This is that rare old bird, a sixteen-line sonnet, following the example of the poet George Meredith, no less.

Critical soundbites

In this demanding revision activity, students must match the following excerpts from criticism to the poet whose work they describe. [Answers are at the end of this book]. In an added twist for this second volume, some of the sound bites come from the poets themselves...

1. 'Their subject is dramatic personae, men and women. There never was for this poet any other subject.'

2. The world this writer imagines is 'full of solid objects and hard edges – stones – wood, frozen ground – which offer little purchase to its inhabitants'.

3. Their 'poetry is known for its aural beauty and finely-wrought textures. Often described as a regional poet,' they are 'also a traditionalist who deliberately gestures back towards the "pre-modern" worlds.

4. 'The traumatic issues' this poet 'grappled with during their childhood — death, mental illness, loneliness, and disillusionment — became themes in their poetry and stories.'

5. 'He created an immensely popular Romantic hero—defiant, melancholy, haunted by secret guilt—for which, to many, he seemed the model. He is also a Romantic paradox: a leader of the era's poetic revolution, he named Alexander Pope as his master; a worshiper of the ideal, he never lost touch with reality.'

6. This poet ignored 'trends and fashions, preferring instead to use traditional forms and to create readable poetry'.

7. 'The major themes are there in this poet's 'dramatic if short life and in his works, enigmatic, inspiring, and lasting: the restlessness and brooding, the rebellion against authority, the interchange with nature, the power of the visionary imagination and of poetry, the pursuit of ideal love, and the untamed spirit ever in search of freedom'.

8. This poet's 'humane and liberal point of view manifests itself' in their 'poems aimed at redressing many forms of social injustice, such as the slave trade in America, the labour of children in the mines and the mills of England, the oppression of the Italian people by the Austrians, and the restrictions forced upon women in nineteenth-century society.'

9. This poet 'maps the complexity of a hybrid belonging, when one is caught among identities, languages, cultural practices and racial categories'.

10. This poet's 'themes include language and the representation of reality; the construction of the self; gender issues; contemporary culture; and many different forms of alienation, oppression and social inequality. [they write] in everyday, conversational language, making their poems appear deceptively simple.'

11. This poet's work rises 'lyrically out of landscape and as if memory itself is a landscape, ranging through love, history, family and the political undercurrents of ordinary life'.

12. This poet's 'carefulness expresses the struggle for balance in the poetry, balance between the competing pressures of his public and private life.' The poet 'once said that' their 'political poems were in fact about love and death'.

13. 'Nor did he seem by nature to be cheerful: much of the criticism around his work concerns its existentially bleak outlook, and, especially during his own time, sexual themes.'

14. This poet's work 'particularly notable for its energy and sensuality, has focused on the way people identify with land and country. There is also an interest in loss, separation and the many different borders that people create between themselves'.

Comparing the poems

Probably the best way to map the relationships between poems in the whole anthology is to set them all out on a large A3 piece of paper and to use colours to draw links between them. This sort of visualisation and the acutal drawing of lines aids retention of information and allows you to have one piece of paper that provides an overview of all the material. Try to link in terms of aspects of love, but also in terms of tones, language and form. For the latter, for instance, interesting comparisons could be made between the sonnets, between different lyrics poems or between dramatic monologues.

If it hasn't already happened in reading the poems, it will quickly become obvious on reviewing them that they fall neatly into two groups - poems about the relationships between lovers and poems about love within family relationships. We don't have to worry about other types of love, such as the patriotic love of country or the love of an idea or ideology. We should, however, bear in mind how on a micro-level relationships between lovers or family members can on a macro-level wider dramatise political relationships.

Between them the poems about the relationships between lovers provide a brief narrative of the process and progress of love as well as of perspectives on relationships. **Shelley**, for instance, outlines the early stages of a desired relationship, in a seduction poem that adeptly mixes spiritual with more physical and erotic elements of love. **Nagra** and the **Brownings** [surely a great name for a literary pop group], both Robert and Elizabeth, take us into the experience and passion of love itself. Like Shelley, Nagra celebrates the erotic dimension of relationships and the bond shared between lovers. In Shelley's poem the whole word is in accord; in Nagra's, however, it offers a contrasting and interfering backdrop. While Elizabeth's poem suggests the dangerous obsessive qualities of love and how, unchecked, it can potentially overwhelm its object, it is a fundamentally positive, celebratory depiction. In contrast, her husband's poem explores those darker suggestions, taking us into the heart and mind of a narrator for whom love has warped and curdled into something horribly, murderously possessive.

Byron, Hardy and Mew take us into the bleak emotional landscapes of the breakdown of relationships and/or the rejection of love. These poems share the pains of heartache, barren and bitter feelings of hurt, sadness, confusion and sometimes hostility. Sheers' and Dooley's poems are also about separation, perhaps between lovers in both cases. In the latter, it is a separation without apparent acrimony and where love may endure. In Sheers' poem, the initial acrimony is transcended and reconciliation captured in the image of swans' wings.

Duffy's poem to her, or her narrator's, mother, shows that the course of family love and relationships also doesn't always run smooth. The jealous, possessive love outlined in this poem links it across the two groups to Browning's and Mew's poems. Armitage offers us another take on the child/mother relationship from the child's perspective, this time a son's. The issues of possessiveness, identity, freedom and constraint crop up again, only, in contrast to Duffy's poem, it is the parent who seems controlling and possessive. Causley also writes from a son's perspective, this time to both parents. As with several other poems in the anthology in both groupings, Causley's poem explores connection and separation. Heaney's *Follower* springs to mind as an apt comparison with a similarly ambivalent take on the child/parent relationship.

Waterhouse's poem, perhaps an elegy, is the only one in the collection written from a grandchild's perspective, but again explores the importance of this figure in terms of the narrator's grip on and of life. In his poem, written from the parent's perspective, *Walking Away*, Lewis memorably calls separation a 'scorching ordeal' and yet, seems to accept, that such experiences are necessary in the forming of individuality and selfhood. A philosophical reflection that might aid all the lovers and beloveds we meet within the anthology as a whole.

149

ALLITERATION – the repetition of consonants at the start of neighbouring words in a line

ANAPAEST - a three beat pattern of syllables, unstress, unstress, stress. E.g. 'on the moon', 'to the coast', 'anapaest'

ANTITHESIS - the use of balanced opposites

APOSTROPHE – a figure of speech addressing a person, object or idea

ASSONANCE – vowel rhyme, e.g. sod and block

BLANK VERSE – unrhymed lines of iambic pentameter

BLAZON – a male lover describing the parts of his beloved

CADENCE – the rise of fall of sounds in a line of poetry

CAESURA – a distinct break in a poetic line, usually marked by punctuation

COMPLAINT – a type of love poem concerned with loss and mourning

CONCEIT – an extended metaphor

CONSONANCE – rhyme based on consonants only, e.g. book and back

COUPLET – a two-line stanza, conventionally rhyming

DACTYL – the reverse pattern to the anapaest; stress, unstress, unstress. E.g. 'Strong as a'

DRAMATIC MONOLOGUE – a poem written in the voice of a distinct character

ELEGY – a poem in mourning for someone dead

END-RHYME – rhyming words at the end of a line

END-STOPPED – the opposite of enjambment; i.e. when the sentence and the poetic line stop at the same point

ENJAMBMENT – where sentences run over the end of lines and stanzas

FIGURATIVE LANGUAGE – language that is not literal, but employs figures of speech, such as metaphor, simile and personification

FEMININE RHYME – a rhyme that ends with an unstressed syllable or unstressed syllables.

FREE VERSE – poetry without metre or a regular, set form

GOTHIC – a style of literature characterised by psychological horror, dark deeds and uncanny events

HEROIC COUPLETS – pairs of rhymed lines in iambic pentameter

HYPERBOLE – extreme exaggeration

IAMBIC – a metrical pattern of a weak followed by a strong stress, ti-TUM, like a heart beat

IMAGERY – the umbrella term for description in poetry. Sensory imagery refers to descriptions that appeal to sight, sound and so forth; figurative imagery refers to the use of devices such as metaphor, simile and personification

JUXTAPOSITION – two things placed together to create a strong contrast

LYRIC – an emotional, personal poem usually with a first-person speaker

MASCULINE RHYME – an end rhyme on a strong syllable

METAPHOR – an implicit comparison in which one thing is said to be another

METAPHYSICAL – a type of poetry characterised by wit and extended metaphors

METRE – the regular pattern organising sound and rhythm in a poem

MOTIF – a repeated image or pattern of language, often carrying thematic significance

OCTET OR OCTAVE – the opening eight lines of a sonnet

ONOMATOPOEIA – bang, crash, wallop

PENTAMETER – a poetic line consisting of five beats

PERSONIFICATION – giving human characteristics to inanimate things

PLOSIVE – a type of alliteration using 'p' and 'b' sounds

QUATRAIN – a four-line stanza

REFRAIN – a line or lines repeated like a chorus

ROMANTIC – A type of poetry characterised by a love of nature, by strong emotion and heightened tone

SESTET – the last six lines in a sonnet

SIMILE – an explicit comparison of two different things

SONNET – a form of poetry with fourteen lines and a variety of possible set rhyme patterns

SPONDEE – two strong stresses together in a line of poetry

STANZA – the technical name for a verse

SYMBOL – something that stands in for something else. Often a concrete representation of an idea.

SYNTAX – the word order in a sentence. doesn't Without sense English syntax make. Syntax is crucial to sense: For example, though it uses all the same words, 'the man eats the fish' is not the same as 'the fish eats the man'

TERCET – a three-line stanza

TETRAMETER – a line of poetry consisting of four beats

TROCHEE – the opposite of an iamb; stress, unstress, strong, weak.

VILLANELLE – a complex interlocking verse form in which lines are recycled

VOLTA – the 'turn' in a sonnet from the octave to the sestet

Recommended reading

Atherton, C., Green, A. & Snapper, G. Teaching English Literature 16-19. NATE, 2013

Bowen et al. The Art of Poetry, vol.1-6. Peripeteia Press, 2015-17

Brinton, I. Contemporary Poetry. CUP, 2009

Eagleton, T. How to Read a Poem. Wiley & Sons, 2006

Fry, S. The Ode Less Travelled. Arrow, 2007

Hamilton, I. & Noel-Todd, J. Oxford Companion to Modern Poetry, OUP, 2014

Herbert, W. & Hollis, M. Strong Words. Bloodaxe, 2000

Meally, M. & Bowen, N. The Art of Writing English Literature Essays, Peripeteia Press, 2014

Maxwell, G. On Poetry. Oberon Masters, 2012

Padel, R. 52 Ways of Looking at a Poem. Vintage, 2004

Padel, R. The Poem and the Journey. Vintage, 2008

Paulin, T. The Secret Life of Poems. Faber & Faber, 2011

Schmidt, M. Lives of the Poets, Orion, 1998

Wolosky, S. The Art of Poetry: How to Read a Poem. OUP, 2008.

About the authors

Head of English and freelance writer, Neil Bowen has a Masters Degree in Literature & Education from Cambridge University and is a member of Ofqual's experts panel for English. He is the author of The Art of Writing English Essays for GCSE, co-author of The Art of Writing English Essays for A-level and Beyond and of The Art of Poetry, volumes 1-7. Neil runs the peripeteia project, bridging the gap between A-level and degree level English courses: www.peripeteia.webs.com.

Neil Jones is an English teacher with a PhD in English Literature from Oxford University, where he specialised in modern poetry.

After completing an English Literature degree at Cambridge University, Jack May began a career in journalism and currently he is working as a sub-editor for a national newspaper.

Kathrine Mortimore is a Lead Practitioner at Torquay Academy. She has a Masters degree in Advanced Subject Teaching from Cambridge University where she focused on tackling disadvantage in the English classroom, a topic she has continued to blog about at: kathrinemortimore.wordpress.com

Answers to critical soundbites:

1. Browning, R.
2. Waterhouse
3. Heaney
4. Mew
5. Byron
6. Causley

7. Shelley

8. Barrett Browning

9. Nagra

10. Duffy

11. Dooley

12. Day Lewis

13. Hardy

14. Sheers

A final revision task: Students create their own anonymised critical sound bites. The class should match the sound bite to the poet/ poem.

Critical sound bites adapted from:

The Cambridge Introduction to Modern Irish Poetry, 1800-200

https://literature.britishcouncil.org

http://www.warpoets.org/

http://www.poetryfoundation.org

http://www.theguardian.com

52 Ways of Looking at a Poem, Ruth Padel

Oxford Companion to Modern Poetry, Hamilton & Noel-Todd

Cambridge Introduction to British Poetry 1945-2010, Eric Falci

Printed in Great Britain
by Amazon